MW01153920

The My Little Pony 2009-2012 Collector's Inventory

an unofficial illustrated MLP guide including all ponies, playsets and accessories
released from 2009 through 2012

by

Summer Hayes

Priced Nostalgia Press ~ New Jersey

All rights reserved. With the exception of quoting brief passages for the purposes of review, no part of this publication may be reproduced without prior written permission from the publisher. Any reproduction of this work without permission of the publisher is prohibited.

The information in this book is true and complete to the best of our knowledge. All information is offered without any guarantee on the part of the author or publisher, who also disclaim any liability incurred in connection with the use of this guide.

We recognize that My Little Pony, *My Little Pony: Friendship is Magic* and all pony, set, character, and playset names are the exclusive property of Hasbro, Inc. and are used without permission for identification purposes only. This is not an official publication, nor is it affiliated with Hasbro in any way. The toys featured in this book are from the private collection of the author and other collectors.

Additional copies of this book are available at www.PricedNostalgia.com.

Library of Congress Control Number: 2013910884

Hayes, Summer. The My Little Pony 2009-2012 Collector's Inventory: an unofficial illustrated MLP guide including all ponies, playsets and accessories released from 2009 through 2012. 1st ed. New Jersey: Priced Nostalgia Press, 2013.

ISBN-10: 0982400322
ISBN-13: 9780982400326

Copyright 2013 Priced Nostalgia

All photographs in this guide were taken by Summer Hayes of items in her private collection unless otherwise indicated below.

Additional Photo Credits

While I took the majority of the photos for this guide, the following people graciously donated photographs for this project. Angie Gouge donated the photos of Rarity's Carousel Boutique bonus accessories. Linda Murphy (Halicabi) supplied photos of the French Ponyville singles and the Core Seven Bucket Pack. She also provided additional accessory information and graciously answered questions about accessory color variations. Sandi supplied the Fluttershy set 6 blind bag trading card photo. Pangel provided loose photos of Fluttershy's Train Car. KaibaGirl007 supplied the photo of the Newborn Cuties two pack. Snapdragon donated photos of the Brazil/Mexican McDonald's Ponies as well as the 2011 Advent Calendar. BerryMouse supplied the 2009 Pinkie Pie in Egg photo and Sora provided a photo of Potty Time with StarSong. Special thanks also go to Rachel Lum of The Olde Video Shoppe for the photo of *The World's Biggest Tea Party* DVD. I'd also like to thank Sebby6 for helping me track down all of those pesky G3 mint in box European exclusive ponies I was missing and for searching through international Ebay auctions and sending me links for missing collection items. Thank you so very much!

Table of Contents

Miniatures

So Soft

2010..57

Ponies and Playsets

Ponyville

Miniatures

So Soft and Plush

2011 81

Ponies and Playsets

Miniatures

So Soft and Plush

2012...113

Ponies and Playsets

Miniatures

So Soft and Plush

Trading Cards 149

5 in

Dress Up   New Look   Newborn Cuties   FiM Style

2.5 in

Original Ponyville   New Look Ponyville   Mermaid Ponyville   Dolly Mix   Blind Bag Miniature

Introduction

My Little Pony underwent many changes between 2009 and 2012 including three distinctively different designs and the launch of a new animated television series, *My Little Pony: Friendship is Magic*, that brought new fans to the brand. This book picks up where *The My Little Pony 2007-2008 Collector's Inventory* left off and covers all ponies, playsets, and miniatures released to date.

The beginning of 2009 continued the 2008 Core Seven focus on just seven pony characters: Cheerilee, Pinkie Pie, Rainbow Dash, Scootaloo, StarSong, Sweetie Belle, and Toola-Roola. It also marked the continuation of the Dress-Up pose that allowed any pony with a particular hanger hoof symbol to wear special molded plastic outfits. But by mid-2009, Hasbro retired the Dress Up ponies and introduced a new design called New Look.

New Look ponies were smaller than previous G3 ponies with larger eyes, small mouths and chubby legs. Some collectors refer to New Look ponies as G3.5 because their appearance was so different from everything that had come before. Pony packaging also got a makeover with new bright pink boxes. While the focus on only the Core Seven characters continued into this new design, New Look ponies were released in multiple body poses and some had removable hair pieces or interchangeable wigs for a variety of different looks.

In addition to the New Look redesign, Hasbro introduced a new line of baby ponies called Newborn Cuties. With painted-on diapers and tiny sewn-on bows in their hair, each Newborn Cutie was a Core Seven character in baby form. The New Look style also came to Ponyville in 2009 and in 2010 Ponyville went under the Sea with a Mermaid theme, though both of these new looks were still limited the Core Seven characters.

October 10th, 2010 was a turning point for the My Little Pony brand with the premiere of *My Little Pony: Friendship is Magic*, a new animated television series developed for Hasbro by Lauren Faust (*The Powerpuff Girls, Foster's Home for Imaginary Friends*). *My Little Pony: Friendship is Magic* gained unexpected adult fans including male fans who called themselves "Bronies" (a combination of "bro" and "ponies") who helped rocket the show into mainstream popularity. The result was an explosion of new ponies and other licensed items that increased exponentially since the show's premiere.

In early 2011, Hasbro gave the My Little Pony toy line a complete overhaul to match the new show. Ponies were now just under 4 inches high with new thinner faces and a new line of miniature ponies, many of which were originally released in Blind Bag sets, replaced Ponyville. To distinguish *My Little Pony: Friendship is Magic* items from everything that came before, some fans of the show began calling items in the new style G4.

This newest reincarnation of My Little Pony introduced a hybrid of new and old characters and the kingdom of Equestria, a new realm that the ponies called home. As the third generation continued from New Look into the *My Little Pony: Friendship is Magic* style, a few characters underwent changes both major and minor. Several ponies changed colors, rump symbols (now called "cutie marks"), species, personalities and even ages to keep continuity with the animated series. While the show focused on the Mane 6 characters (Twilight Sparkle, Fluttershy, Rarity, Pinkie Pie, Rainbow Dash and Applejack), the toy line featured a variety of other characters as well, a welcome relief for collectors weary of years of only Core Seven ponies.

The My Little Pony items in this book are organized according to the year in which they were released. Each year is then broken down into sets. An index is provided in the back to assist the reader when searching for a specific pony or set.

Because there are multiple versions of some of the MLP characters in different body poses, I have added a Roman numeral after some pony names to denote which pose the pony is in. If no Roman numeral appears, the Roman numeral I is implied. This numbering system refers only to the molded pose of the pony and not the markings or other external decorations. Roman numerals continue from my previous books into this one but start over for full sized New Look ponies, *My Little Pony: Friendship is Magic* style, and the new Blind Bag style miniature ponies.

Each pony is pictured with an accompanying checklist to help organize your collection. All items in this book were photographed immediately after being removed from their packaging. Ponies were not styled as I wished the photos to reflect their factory condition. Accessories are included in pony photographs and accessory colors are listed whenever possible.

I hope you find this guide helpful while organizing your My Little Pony collection!

~Summer Hayes

2009

Core Seven Friends

This set of Core Seven ponies was one of the final sets to use the original G3 body molds. Each pony's body featured additional accents unique to her personality. All ponies in this set were in the Dress-Up pose (indicated by a hanger symbol on their foreleg) which allowed them to share accessories and clothing with other Dress-Up pose ponies. Ponies were packaged with a single accessory and did not come with brushes.

- ❏ **Cheerilee**
  - ❏ Yellow butterfly cowboy hat

- ❏ **Pinkie Pie VII**
  - ❏ Yellow tiara
- ❏ **Rainbow Dash IV**
  - ❏ Pink purse

- ❏ **Scootaloo II**
  - ❏ Purple tennis racquet
- ❏ **StarSong**
  - ❏ Pink radio

- ❏ **Sweetie Belle**
  - ❏ Pink and purple swirl lollipop
- ❏ **Toola-Roola**
  - ❏ Yellow painting pallet

Discount Store Ponies

Four of the Core Seven ponies were sold in Big Lots, Family Dollar and other discount stores. While Cheerilee and Rainbow Dash were identical to previous versions, Pinkie Pie and Sweetie Belle had slight differences that made them unique. Pinkie Pie's cutie mark was on the right side of her body and Sweetie Belle's was on her left. Each pony was accompanied with a brush.

❑ **Cheerilee**
 ❑ Dark pink bow brush

❑ **Pinkie Pie VII**
 ❑ Pink bow brush

❑ **Rainbow Dash IV**
 ❑ Blue bow brush

❑ **Sweetie Belle**
 ❑ White bow brush

Easter Egg and Pony

Available exclusively in the United Kingdom, this set contained Cheerilee and a large edible milk chocolate egg. Cheerilee has gradient coloring on her back leg and is identical to her 2008 Spring Pony release. **Collector's Note:** The milk chocolate egg will melt if not stored correctly. Collectors should consider either removing the egg from the packaging or otherwise storing the mint in box set in a cool location.

- ❑ **Cheerilee**
- ❑ Bunny ears with yellow
- ❑ Milk chocolate egg

Pony Dress-Up Sets

Sharing the same Dress-Up pose, each pony could fit into specially molded clothing pieces and share them with any other pony in the Dress-Up pose. Each pony was accompanied with a variety of themed accessories. Dancin' Fun StarSong hit some store shelves in late 2008, but it wasn't until early 2009 that she became widely available.

Dancin' Fun with StarSong
- ❑ **StarSong**
- ❑ Yellow dress
- ❑ Pink dress
- ❑ Green radio
- ❑ 4 dark pink ballet slippers
- ❑ 4 blue ballet slippers
- ❑ Pink and purple headband
- ❑ Pale pink ballet bar and mirror

(**Variation:** dark pink)

Available in parts of Europe and Canada in 2008 and 2009, these hard-to-find bonus sets contained extra accessories for your Dress-Up pony. Two different bonus packs were available for Pinkie Pie, each containing different bonus accessories. The outfits packaged with the main pony are the same as those in the original 2008 Dress-Up sets with some color variations while the ponies are all reissues.

Arts & Crafts with Toola-Roola Bonus Pack
- ❑ **Toola-Roola**
- ❑ Yellow shirt
- ❑ Green skirt
- ❑ Pink painter's smock
- ❑ Light blue shorts
- ❑ Pink beret
- ❑ 4 green tennis shoes
- ❑ Pink paintbrush
- ❑ Yellow palette
- ❑ Pink easel with green tray
- ❑ 2 large paintings
- ❑ 1 small painting
- ❑ Bonus white and pink shirt
- ❑ Bonus white and pink skirt
- ❑ Bonus 4 pink shoes

Go to School with Cheerilee Bonus Pack
- ❑ **Cheerilee**
- ❑ Light pink shirt
- ❑ Orange skirt
- ❑ Green shirt
- ❑ Green and pink pleated skirt
- ❑ 4 pink and white shoes
- ❑ Pink pompom
- ❑ Green headband
- ❑ Pink desk with orange top
- ❑ Orange book
- ❑ Yellow barrette
- ❑ Orange barrette
- ❑ Bonus purple and pink shirt
- ❑ Bonus pink skirt
- ❑ Bonus purple shoes

Pinkie Pie's Party Bonus Pack Version 1
- ❑ **Pinkie Pie VII**
- ❑ Blue shirt
- ❑ Pink skirt
- ❑ Pink shirt
- ❑ Blue skirt
- ❑ 4 purple shoes
- ❑ Pink party hat
- ❑ Light pink cake with green candles
- ❑ Cake slice
- ❑ 2 greeting cards
- ❑ Bonus pink shirt
- ❑ Bonus pink skirt
- ❑ Bonus 4 pink and white shoes

Pinkie Pie's Party Bonus Pack Version 2
- ❑ **Pinkie Pie VII**
- ❑ Pink shirt with white trim
- ❑ 2 pink skirts
- ❑ Pink shirt
- ❑ 4 green shoes
- ❑ Pink party hat
- ❑ Blue cake with orange candles
- ❑ Cake slice
- ❑ 2 greeting cards
- ❑ Bonus white shirt
- ❑ Bonus blue skirt
- ❑ Bonus 4 pink shoes

Rainbow Dash's Special Day

This version of Rainbow Dash came wearing a Dress-Up outfit and packaged with a copy of *Rainbow Dash's Special Day* DVD.

Rainbow Dash's Special Day
- ❑ **Rainbow Dash IV**
- ❑ *Rainbow Dash's Special Day* DVD
- ❑ Pink and yellow shirt
- ❑ Pink skirt
- ❑ Pink tiara
- ❑ 4 yellow shoes

Spring Pinkie Pie

Available exclusively in France for a limited time, this set is hard to find.

- ❑ **Pinkie Pie VII**
- ❑ Yellow pie
- ❑ Pie server
- ❑ Purple tiara
- ❑ Butterfly brush
- ❑ Pink tote bag

Spring Ponies

This year's spring themed pony set contained only two ponies both of which were Core Seven characters in the Dress-Up pose: Cheerilee and Rainbow Dash. Though their packages resembled baskets and they wore bunny ears, neither pony had any unusual physical features to designate them as Spring Ponies.

- ❑ **Cheerilee II**
- ❑ Blue bunny ears

- ❑ **Rainbow Dash IV**
- ❑ Pink bunny ears

Valentine's Day Ponies

Both 2009 Valentine's Day ponies came in the Dress-Up pose and were Core Seven characters. In addition to their usual cutie marks, these ponies had additional heart designs on their bodies. Each Valentine's Day pony came packaged with a bow brush.

❑ **Pinkie Pie VII**
  ❑ Pink bow brush

❑ **Sweetie Belle**
  ❑ White bow brush

New Look Core 7 Ponies

In the latter half of 2009, Hasbro gave My Little Pony's body design an overhaul with new poses called New Look. These ponies were markedly smaller than previous pony molds standing between 4 and 6 inches high. They featured chunky feet, larger eyes, and small mouths. Each pony had her own signature hairstyle and came packaged with a brush.

❑ **Cheerilee**
  ❑ Dark pink brush

❑ **Pinkie Pie**
  ❑ Pink brush

❑ **Rainbow Dash**
  ❑ Blue brush

❑ **Scootaloo**
  ❑ Orange brush

❑ **StarSong**
  ❑ Purple brush

❑ **Sweetie Belle**
  ❑ White brush

❑ **Toola-Roola**
  ❑ Pale pink brush

Dress-Up Sets

Much like the earlier Dress-Up Sets, each pony in this set was accompanied by a variety of themed accessories. In addition to multiple outfits, ponies also came with molded wigs that were interchangeable between other New Look ponies of the same style.

Pinkie Pie's Dress Up

- ☐ **Pinkie Pie**
- ☐ Bright yellow teddy bear
- ☐ Plate of green muffins
- ☐ Plate of pink cookies
- ☐ Pink shirt with white sleeves
- ☐ Pink wig with blue hat
- ☐ Pink wig
- ☐ Pink pleated skirt
- ☐ Dark pink skirt
- ☐ Pink skirt
- ☐ White shirt
- ☐ Dark pink shirt
- ☐ 4 blue shoes
- ☐ Yellow teapot
- ☐ 2 blue teacups
- ☐ White purse

Scootaloo's Dress Up

- ❏ **Scootaloo**
- ❏ Pink and purple wig with cowboy hat
- ❏ Pink and purple wig with chef hat
- ❏ Pink shirt with light pink trim
- ❏ Pink shirt with green trim
- ❏ Pink skirt
- ❏ Long pink skirt
- ❏ Yellow pants
- ❏ Dark pink shirt
- ❏ 4 pink boots
- ❏ 4 white shoes
- ❏ Green glasses

Hair Play Ponies

With a variety of interchangeable wigs, these ponies could easily change hairstyles to create new looks.

Cheerilee's Hairstyles

- ❏ **Cheerilee II**
- ❏ Molded wig with curlers
- ❏ Molded wig with pigtails
- ❏ Molded wig with up do
- ❏ Purple cucumber eye mask
- ❏ Green and purple hair dryer
- ❏ Purple comb

Lots-of-Styles StarSong

- ❏ **StarSong**
- ❏ 2 brushable curly pigtails
- ❏ 2 molded pigtails
- ❏ 2 molded braids
- ❏ Purple star comb
- ❏ Purple star barrette

Pony Pack

Available exclusively at Target stores, this two pack contained Rainbow Dash and Pinkie Pie wearing scarves and covered with designs similar to the G1 Twice as Fancy Ponies.

- ❑ **Pinkie Pie**
- ❑ **Rainbow Dash**
- ❑ Blue scarf
- ❑ Pink scarf
- ❑ Pink brush

Positively Pink

This DVD of *Positively Pink* starring Pinkie Pie included the star herself.

- ❑ **Pinkie Pie**
- ❑ *Positively Pink* DVD
- ❑ Pink brush

RC Scootaloo on the Go

Repackaged with the same remote control scooter as the 2008 Scootaloo on the Go, the New Look version of Scootaloo had the new pink style packaging.

- ❑ **Scootaloo**
- ❑ Pink scooter
- ❑ Remote control
- ❑ Pink helmet

Sparkly Ponies

Similar to the Sparkle Ponies of early 2000, Sparkly Ponies had glitter on their cutie marks, tinsel in their manes and the added feature that their names were printed along their sides. This set included all of the Core Seven characters except Toola-Roola. Each came packaged with a brush and activity book.

- ❏ **Cheerilee**
  - ❏ Dark pink brush
  - ❏ Activity book
- ❏ **Pinkie Pie**
  - ❏ Pink brush
  - ❏ Activity book

- ❏ **Rainbow Dash**
  - ❏ Blue brush
  - ❏ Activity book
- ❏ **Scootaloo**
  - ❏ Orange brush
  - ❏ Activity book

- ❏ **StarSong**
  - ❏ Purple brush
  - ❏ Activity book
- ❏ **Sweetie Belle**
  - ❏ White brush
  - ❏ Activity book

Styling Pony Pinkie Pie

This 8" version of New Look Pinkie Pie had a long mane and tail and included a variety of styling accessories.

- ❑ **Pinkie Pie**
- ❑ Blue and yellow balloon hair clip
- ❑ Purple heart and balloon barrette
- ❑ 2 pink star barrettes
- ❑ Yellow heart barrette
- ❑ Purple hair dryer
- ❑ Pink balloon comb

Super Long Hair Ponies

These Super Long Hair Ponies have long hair that you can style or interchange with other hair pieces to create new looks.

- ❑ **Cheerilee**
- ❑ 2 long brushable pigtails
- ❑ 2 shorter brushable pigtails
- ❑ 2 molded braided pigtails
- ❑ Pink flower comb

❑ **Rainbow Dash**
❑ 2 rainbow and cloud hair clips
❑ Pink bow barrette
❑ White rainbow and cloud comb

Winter Ponies

While previous Winter Ponies were released in sets of three, 2009 had only one lone Winter Pony in the New Look pose. Sweetie Belle's packaging resembled a snow globe.

❑ **Sweetie Belle**
❑ 3 blue snowflake barrettes
❑ Blue snowflake comb
❑ Scarf

Art Ponies

Continuing their line of ponies aimed at adult collectors, Hasbro created both the Pop and Underwater Art Ponies. Each pony was packaged in a square Art Pony box and sold exclusively through the Hasbro Toy Shop website and other specialty stores. The Pop Pony was covered in artistic abstract designs while the Underwater Pony was covered with fish, seaweed, and bubbles.

❑ **Pop Art Pony**

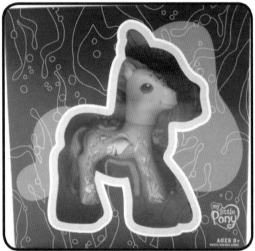 

❑ **Underwater Art Pony**

Junko Mizuno Art Pony

Modeled after the 18-inch pony designed by international artist Junko Mizuno that was auctioned off for charity as part of the "The MY LITTLE PONY PROJECT: 25 Ponies for 25 Years," this unusual pony was produced in a smaller scale for collectors as part of the Art Pony line. The Junko Mizuno Pony came in a square Art Pony box and sold exclusively through the Hasbro Toy Shop website and other specialty stores. Her body was decorated with flames, an octopus-like creature, a painted bodice with a girl's head and flowers.

❑ **Junko Mizuno Art Pony**
❑ Faux fur hood with tassels
❑ 4 clear shoes with pink flowers

2009 San Diego Comic Con Pony

Available exclusively to attendees of the San Diego Comic Convention (often abbreviated SDCC), this superhero themed pony had dueling personalities. Her hero side sported a mask and brightly painted costume. The word "WHAM" ran

up her hind leg while her cutie mark was a speech bubble promising, "I'LL SAVE THE DAY!" Her villain side had darker body and eye colors. That cutie mark speech bubble read, "I'LL RULE THE WORLD!" while the word "GRRR" ran up her hind leg. This two faced pony came in a square Art Pony box.

❏ **2009 SDCC Pony**

2009 Convention Exclusive Peacock Art Pony

Offered exclusively to attendees of the 2009 My Little Pony Conventions including the US My Little Pony Fair in Las Vegas and the UK Ponycon in Sheffield, the Peacock Art Pony has no official name. She came packaged in a square Art Pony box.

❏ **2009 Convention Exclusive Peacock Art Pony**

Newborn Cuties

The newest arrivals to the My Little Pony family, Newborn Cuties, were the essence of cute. With cherubic features, painted on diapers and soft curly hair, each Newborn Cutie came packaged with two baby accessories and a bow.

- ❑ **Cheerilee**
  - ❑ Mint green bow
  - ❑ Muffin with purple wrapper
  - ❑ Yellow cookies

- ❑ **Pinkie Pie**
  - ❑ Blue bow
  - ❑ Yellow and purple winter hat
  - ❑ Yellow scarf

- ❑ **Rainbow Dash**
  - ❑ Bright pink bow
  - ❑ Pink rain coat
  - ❑ Yellow duck

- ❑ **Scootaloo**
  - ❑ Greenish yellow bow
  - ❑ Pink hat
  - ❑ Purple bunny toy

- ❑ **StarSong**
  - ❑ Yellow bow
  - ❑ Pink birthday hat
  - ❑ Yellow balloon

- ❑ **Toola-Roola**
  - ❑ Bright pink bow
  - ❑ White hat
  - ❑ Purple blocks

Newborn Cuties 2-pack

Packaged in a vinyl butterfly shaped case, this set included new versions of Cheerilee and Scootaloo with painted on clothing and multiple accessories.

- ❑ **Cheerilee**
- ❑ **Scootaloo**
- ❑ Bright green bow
- ❑ Blue bow
- ❑ Pink balloons with aqua strings (**Variation:** orange strings)
- ❑ Yellow sun hat
- ❑ Green winter hat
- ❑ Purple bunny toy
- ❑ Orange giraffe toy (**Variations:** green or aqua)
- ❑ Purple wagon with green wheels and handle (**Variation:** orange handle)

Newborn Cuties Sets

From feeding to bathing to playtime, these accessory sets included everything you'd need to take care of the Newborn Cuties.

Bubble Time with Cheerilee
- ❑ **Cheerilee**
- ❑ Yellow bow
- ❑ Pink bathtub with shower
- ❑ Yellow and pink clothes hamper
- ❑ Blue shower cap
- ❑ White towel

Bubble Time with Toola-Roola
- ❑ **Toola-Roola**
- ❑ Bright pink bow
- ❑ Purple bathtub
- ❑ Purple and pink clothes hamper
- ❑ Blue shower cap
- ❑ White towel

Feeding Time with Pinkie Pie
- ❑ **Pinkie Pie**
- ❑ Blue bow
- ❑ Yellow and purple highchair
- ❑ Blue feeding dish
- ❑ Cereal box
- ❑ Pink bowl

Feeding Time with Scootaloo
- ❑ **Scootaloo**
- ❑ Pink bow
- ❑ Purple and pink highchair
- ❑ Blue feeding dish
- ❑ Cereal box
- ❑ Pink bowl

Nap Time with Cheerilee
- ❑ **Cheerilee**
- ❑ Yellow bow
- ❑ Purple crib with mobile
- ❑ Orange book
- ❑ Pink pony doll

Play Time with StarSong
- ❑ **StarSong**
- ❑ Pink bow
- ❑ Pink bassinet
- ❑ Purple elephant toy
- ❑ Blue keys
- ❑ Orange rattle

Scootaloo's Party
- ❑ **Scootaloo**
- ❑ Greenish yellow bow
- ❑ Pink birthday cake
- ❑ Pink party hat
- ❑ Dark pink and purple gift box
- ❑ Yellow and pink balloons

Strolling Along with Sweetie Belle
- ❑ **Sweetie Belle**
- ❑ Pink bow
- ❑ Pink, yellow, and purple baby buggy with attached bottle
- ❑ Green diaper bag
- ❑ Purple hat

Potty Time with StarSong
- ❑ **StarSong**
- ❑ Pink bow
- ❑ Pink potty chair
- ❑ Aqua soap dispenser
- ❑ Orange book

Newborn Cuties Mom and Me Sets

Family Convertible

Pinkie Pie and her mother arrived in style in this pink pony convertible complete with a car seat for Pinkie Pie's safety. This Newborn Cuties Pinkie Pie does not have blush on her cheeks.

- ❑ **Pinkie Pie's Mom**
- ❑ **Pinkie Pie**
- ❑ Blue bow
- ❑ Pink convertible car
- ❑ Purple car seat
- ❑ Purple bag of groceries
- ❑ Green lunch box
- ❑ Orange to-go cup

Shopping Day with Mom

This set included a shopping cart with a built in seat for Little Rainbow Dash. The cart attaches to Mom's leg so she can push it while picking out groceries.

- ❑ **Rainbow Dash's Mom**
- ❑ **Rainbow Dash**
- ❑ Pink bow
- ❑ Pink and yellow shopping cart
- ❑ Watermelon
- ❑ Bananas
- ❑ Pink bottle

Newborn Cuties Playsets

Little Rainbow Dash's Room

This nursery themed playset included a unique crawling version of Rainbow Dash that came with several baby accessories.

- ❑ **Rainbow Dash**
- ❑ Orange bow
- ❑ Pink crib with mobile
- ❑ Green riding toy
- ❑ Blue book
- ❑ Pink pony doll
- ❑ Pink blanket printed with rainbows

At Toys R Us stores, Little Rainbow Dash's Room included a bonus Newborn Cuties Cheerilee and accessories in a Special Value Pack. Cheerilee's diaper design was unique to this set.

- ❑ **Cheerilee**
- ❑ Blue bow
- ❑ Yellow blanket printed with flowers
- ❑ Pink hat

Pinkie Pie's Playhouse

This large battery operated playset featured interactive elements including a working light, spinning fan, and flushable potty.

- ❏ **Pinkie Pie**
- ❏ Mint green bow
- ❏ Pink crib
- ❏ Pink swing with base
- ❏ Blue flower bottle
- ❏ Yellow pull dog toy
- ❏ Orange bear
- ❏ Green feeding dish

At Toys R Us stores, Pinkie Pie's Playhouse included bonus accessories and Newborn Cuties Rainbow Dash and StarSong in a Special Value Pack. Rainbow Dash and StarSong were the same as the versions released individually.

- ❏ **Rainbow Dash**
- ❏ **StarSong**
- ❏ Bright pink bow
- ❏ Pink bow
- ❏ Purple blocks
- ❏ Pink birthday hat
- ❏ Yellow balloon
- ❏ Pink winter hat
- ❏ White hat

Celebrate Spring with Cheerilee and Toola-Roola

Packaged with spring themed accessories and a wig with bunny ears, this set contained two Ponyville Ponies.

❑ **Cheerilee II**
❑ **Toola-Roola III**
❑ Pink and yellow butterfly
❑ White bunny
❑ Blue bouquet of flowers with card
❑ Pink purse
❑ Yellow skirt
❑ Orange shopping bag
❑ Pink, yellow, and orange wig with bunny ears
❑ Pink wig with green bows

Ferris Wheel

This musical moving Ferris Wheel originally came packaged with the Sweet Sundae Amusement Park in 2008 but sold on its own in 2009 with additions like brightly colored ice cream cars, a purple base, and a brighter color scheme. The Pinkie Pie pony and packaging for this set are the first of several that mimic the New Look style and interchangable wigs of the full size ponies from this year.

❑ **Pinkie Pie**
❑ Pink pigtails wig with blue bows

Hairstyles in a Snap Ponyville Singles

Each pony in this set came in the New Look style and was packaged with a small accessory. Hasbro released two versions of Cheerilee, Pinkie Pie, Rainbow Dash, and StarSong each wearing different interchangeable wigs. Scootaloo and Sweetie Belle were sold with only one hairstyle and were available only in France.

❑ **Cheerilee VII**
❑ Pink wig with pigtails
❑ White and pink wings

❑ **Cheerilee VII**
❑ **Variation:** Pink wig with hair down
❑ White and pink wings

❑ **Pinkie Pie VIII**
❑ Pink wig with hair down
❑ Bright pink balloon

❑ **Pinkie Pie VIII**
❑ **Variation:** Pink wig with up-do
❑ Bright pink balloon

❑ **Rainbow Dash VIII**
❑ Multicolored wig with pigtails
❑ Multicolored pinwheel with pink handle

❑ **Rainbow Dash VIII**
❑ **Variation:** Multicolored wig with up-do
❑ Multicolored pinwheel with pink handle

❑ **StarSong III**
- ❑ Pink wig with up-do
- ❑ White bunny

❑ **StarSong III**
- ❑ **Variation:** Pink wig with hair down
  - ❑ White bunny

❑ **Scootaloo V**
- ❑ Pink and purple wig
- ❑ Bright pink purse

❑ **Sweetie Belle II**
- ❑ Pink and purple wig with pigtails
- ❑ Pink chef hat

Ice Cream Shake Diner

This ice cream float shaped playset folded out to create a diner complete with drive-thru where Scootaloo could serve her favorite treats to her Ponyville friends.

- ❑ **Scootaloo**
- ❑ Aqua and white blender
- ❑ Purple and pink wig
- ❑ White pizza box
- ❑ Pizza with slice
- ❑ Pink carton with french fries
- ❑ White shopping bag
- ❑ Bright pink tray
- ❑ Pink ice cream soda
- ❑ Pink ice cream sundae
- ❑ Pink hat
- ❑ Pink car

La-Ti-Da Hair & Spa

With five different interchangeable Hairstyles in a Snap wigs and multiple accessories, Cheerilee could pamper herself during a day at the spa.

- ❑ **Cheerilee III**
- ❑ Blue bathtub
- ❑ Orange shoe box
- ❑ Pink shoe box
- ❑ 4 pink shoes
- ❑ 4 green shoes
- ❑ Green and yellow wig
- ❑ Pink and purple wig
- ❑ Pink wig
- ❑ Orange wig
- ❑ Blue bottle
- ❑ White hairbrush
- ❑ Pink hair dryer
- ❑ Pink and yellow scissors
- ❑ Blue hanger
- ❑ White hanger
- ❑ Yellow skirt
- ❑ Green skirt

La-Ti-Da Hair & Spa Special Edition

Available exclusively at Kohl's stores and packaged in the new pink style box with additional accessories, alternate colors, and multiple ponies all in the New Look pose, this set provided even more opportunities to pamper your ponies.

- ❑ **Pinkie Pie VIII**
- ❑ **Sweetie Belle II**
- ❑ **Rainbow Dash VIII**
- ❑ Orange and yellow wig
- ❑ Pink and purple pigtails wig
- ❑ Pink, purple, and dark purple pigtails wig
- ❑ Pink wig
- ❑ Pink hair down wig
- ❑ Pink and purple hair down wig
- ❑ Multicolored up-do wig
- ❑ Aqua bathtub
- ❑ Orange shoe box
- ❑ Blue shoe box
- ❑ White bottle
- ❑ Orange hairbrush
- ❑ Yellow and pink scissors
- ❑ White hanger
- ❑ Yellow hanger
- ❑ Yellow skirt
- ❑ Orange skirt
- ❑ Green skirt
- ❑ Pink skirt
- ❑ White vanity

Pinkie Pie with Puzzle

This 24 piece puzzle came packaged with Pinkie Pie in a plastic cylinder. The first release of this set had Pinkie Pie in the original Ponyville style with molded hair. A second version of this set arrived in late 2009 with a New Look style Pinkie Pie wearing a wig.

❑ **Pinkie Pie**
❑ Puzzle

❑ **Variation: Pinkie Pie VIII**
❑ Pink wig
❑ Puzzle

Ponyville 3-Pack

Available exclusively at Target stores, this set included three Ponyville ponies in the original style with interchangeable wigs and multiple accessories.

- ❏ **Pinkie Pie V**
- ❏ **Scootaloo**
- ❏ **StarSong II**
- ❏ Pink balloons
- ❏ Orange and pink cake
- ❏ Pink table
- ❏ Pink teapot
- ❏ Light blue tray
- ❏ Yellow creamer
- ❏ Yellow sugar bowl
- ❏ Pink plate with cookies
- ❏ 2 yellow cups with saucers
- ❏ Pink frosted cupcakes
- ❏ Purple ponytail wig
- ❏ Pink pigtails wig
- ❏ Pink wig

Ponyville Adventure Game

Available exclusively at Target stores, this Milton Bradley board game came packaged in a zippered storage case. Four original style Ponyville figures acted as the game pieces.

- ❏ **Toola-Roola**
- ❏ **Scootaloo**
- ❏ **Sweetie Belle**
- ❏ **Pinkie Pie II**

Ponyville Easter Eggs

Packaged to resemble an egg carton, six Ponyville Ponies in the original style hid inside Easter eggs in this set.

- ❑ **Cheerilee II**
- ❑ Yellow egg
- ❑ **Pinkie Pie II**
- ❑ Blue egg

- ❑ **Rainbow Dash VII**
- ❑ Orange egg
- ❑ **Scootaloo IV**
- ❑ Purple egg

- ❑ **StarSong**
- ❑ Pink egg
- ❑ **Sweetie Belle**
- ❑ Green egg

Ponyville Packs

Each Ponyville Pack included two Ponyville Ponies and a variety of themed accessories. The Ponyville ponies in the first wave of this set have the original style Ponyville body molds with interchangeable wigs.

Hairstyles in a Snap with Rainbow Dash and Toola-Roola

- ❑ **Rainbow Dash III**
- ❑ **Toola-Roola III**
- ❑ White pedestal sink with mirror
- ❑ Pink skirt
- ❑ Green skirt
- ❑ Pink wings
- ❑ Orange wings

- ❑ Yellow bottle
- ❑ Orange bottle
- ❑ Bright pink hand mirror
- ❑ Yellow rubber duck
- ❑ White towel
- ❑ Pink comb
- ❑ Pink, purple, and lavender wig

- ❑ Orange, pink, yellow, and green wig
- ❑ Pink and orange ponytail wig
- ❑ Pink hair down wig
- ❑ Aqua bubbles wig
- ❑ Pink towel wrap wig

Scootin' Along with Pinkie Pie & StarSong

- ❏ **Pinkie Pie V**
- ❏ **StarSong II**
- ❏ Green car
- ❏ Orange scooter
- ❏ Bright pink traffic light
- ❏ Bright pink purse
- ❏ Pink purse
- ❏ Yellow keys
- ❏ Bright pink sunglasses
- ❏ Pink water bottle
- ❏ Pink wig with visor
- ❏ Pink pigtails wig

Snacks with Cheerilee and Scootaloo

- ❏ **Cheerilee III**
- ❏ **Scootaloo III**
- ❏ Green table with white umbrella
- ❏ Light blue hat
- ❏ White hat
- ❏ White milk carton
- ❏ 2 purple cake slices
- ❏ Pink and white ice cream sundae
- ❏ White glass of lemonade
- ❏ Yellow picnic basket
- ❏ Sandwich on a pink plate
- ❏ Light blue pitcher
- ❏ Orange plate of cookies
- ❏ Green apple and yellow banana
- ❏ Pink and white cake
- ❏ Pink bowl of cereal
- ❏ Orange cup
- ❏ White plate of muffins
- ❏ Pink wig
- ❏ Pink and purple pigtails wig

A second wave of Ponyville Packs arrived later this same year with interchangeable wigs and the New Look style and packaging.

Cheerleader Fun with Pinkie Pie and Rainbow Dash

- ❑ **Pinkie Pie VIII**
- ❑ **Rainbow Dash VIII**
- ❑ 2 bright pink pompoms
- ❑ 2 green pompoms
- ❑ Bright pink cheer bag
- ❑ Orange cheer bag
- ❑ Bright pink megaphone
- ❑ Green megaphone
- ❑ Bright pink water bottle
- ❑ Green water bottle
- ❑ Yellow pennant
- ❑ Bright pink baton
- ❑ 2 pink cheerleading skirts
- ❑ 2 orange cheerleading skirts
- ❑ 4 pink shoes
- ❑ 4 orange shoes
- ❑ Orange trophy
- ❑ Orange award medal
- ❑ Pink ponytail wig
- ❑ Pink up-do wig
- ❑ Multicolored up-do wig
- ❑ Multicolored pigtail wig

Cooking Party with Cheerilee & StarSong

- ❑ **Cheerilee VI**
- ❑ **StarSong III**
- ❑ Pink and yellow refrigerator
- ❑ White pizza box
- ❑ Pizza
- ❑ Pizza slice
- ❑ Green plate of brownies
- ❑ Periwinkle cup
- ❑ Blue carton of milk
- ❑ Sandwich on orange plate
- ❑ Yellow bowl of cereal
- ❑ Orange apple and banana
- ❑ Pink half up wig
- ❑ Pink hair down wig

Pizza Night with Cheerilee and StarSong

- ❏ **Cheerilee VI**
- ❏ **StarSong III**
- ❏ Bright pink table
- ❏ Bright pink pizza box
- ❏ Pizza
- ❏ Yellow plate of pasta
- ❏ Yellow drink with straw
- ❏ Orange drink with straw

- ❏ Orange purse
- ❏ Pink fork
- ❏ Orange fork
- ❏ White bowl of noodles
- ❏ Pink bowl of salad
- ❏ Pink plate of dessert
- ❏ White salt and pepper shakers
- ❏ Yellow and orange bread basket

- ❏ Pink skirt
- ❏ White chef hat
- ❏ Pink wig with pigtails
- ❏ Pink hair down wig
- ❏ Pink up-do wig
- ❏ Pink hair down wig

Scootin' Along with Scootaloo and Toola-Roola

- ❏ **Scootaloo V**
- ❏ **Toola-Roola IV**
- ❏ Pink car
- ❏ Green scooter

- ❏ Pink traffic light
- ❏ Pink purse
- ❏ Aqua purse
- ❏ Green keys

- ❏ Blue sunglasses
- ❏ Yellow water bottle
- ❏ Yellow, orange, and pink wig
- ❏ Pink and purple ponytail wig

Scootaloo and Sweetie Belle's Tricycle

- ❑ **Scootaloo V**
- ❑ **Sweetie Belle II**
- ❑ Pink tricycle
- ❑ Purple wagon
- ❑ Light blue lunch box

- ❑ Pink sandwich
- ❑ Red water bottle
- ❑ Yellow juice box
- ❑ 2 purses
- ❑ Ponyville card

- ❑ Pink and purple pigtail wig with yellow helmet
- ❑ Pink and purple ponytail wig with blue and white helmet

Ponyville Singles

With molded clothing, unique poses and the ability to stand upright and hold objects in their hooves, these Ponyville Ponies were more human-like than ever before. Many have an accessory molded to their hooves that is not listed separately. Because of their unique poses, ponies in this set have not been assigned pose numbers.

Bake with Rainbow Dash
- ❑ **Rainbow Dash**
- ❑ Yellow carton of eggs
- ❑ Green mixing bowl
- ❑ Orange spoon
- ❑ Pink pie
- ❑ White cookbook
- ❑ Orange milk carton

Celebrate with Pinkie Pie
- ❑ **Pinkie Pie**
- ❑ Birthday card
- ❑ Yellow serving tray
- ❑ Pink cake slice on green plate
- ❑ White gift box
- ❑ Bright pink cake

Cook with Cheerilee
- ❏ **Cheerilee**
  - ❏ Newspaper
  - ❏ Pink tray with pancakes
  - ❏ Green toaster
  - ❏ Pink frying pan with eggs

Get Pinkie Pie ready for bed
- ❏ **Pinkie Pie**
  - ❏ Pink and blue storybook
  - ❏ Bright pink alarm clock
  - ❏ Pink and white stripped blanket
  - ❏ Green toothpaste and pink toothbrush

Help StarSong Get Pretty
- ❏ **StarSong**
  - ❏ Pink dresser
  - ❏ Yellow hairspray
  - ❏ Yellow spray bottle
  - ❏ Bright pink brush

Paint with Toola-Roola
- ❏ **Toola-Roola**
  - ❏ Pink and orange paint tubes
  - ❏ Yellow artist pallet
  - ❏ Green easel
  - ❏ 2 paintings

Read with Sweetie Belle
- ❏ **Sweetie Belle**
  - ❏ Apple and pink water bottle
  - ❏ Light blue backpack
  - ❏ Orange lamp
  - ❏ Green note pad

Serve Snacks with Sweetie Belle
- ❏ **Sweetie Belle**
  - ❏ White plate and hamburger
  - ❏ Pink carton of french fries
  - ❏ Yellow menu board
  - ❏ Bright pink canned drink with straw

While packaged with the same accessories as the Hairstyles in a Snap Ponyville Singles, this wave of Ponyville Ponies was only available in France.

❑ **Cheerilee**
   ❑ White and pink wings

❑ **Pinkie Pie V**
   ❑ Bright pink balloon

❑ **Rainbow Dash**
   ❑ Multicolored pinwheel with pink handle

❑ **StarSong**
   ❑ White bunny

A final wave of Ponyville Singles arrived later this same year with some big changes. Ponies arrived with all new poses that mimicked the New Look style and packaging of the full sized ponies.

A day in the garden with Sweetie Belle

❑ **Sweetie Belle**
❑ Bright pink and yellow flower pot with flowers
❑ Pink and yellow butterfly
❑ Pink magnifying glass

A day in the park with Pinkie Pie

❑ **Pinkie Pie**
❑ Bright pink popcorn box with popcorn
❑ Light blue and yellow pinwheel
❑ Pink cotton candy

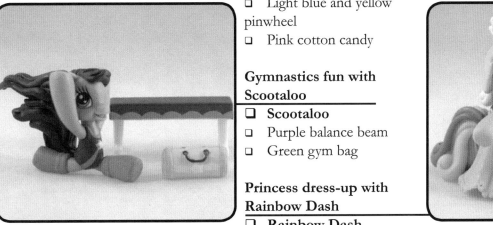

Gymnastics fun with Scootaloo

❑ **Scootaloo**
❑ Purple balance beam
❑ Green gym bag

Princess dress-up with Rainbow Dash

❑ **Rainbow Dash**
❑ Green frog prince
❑ Brown treasure chest

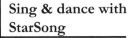

Sing & dance with StarSong

❑ **StarSong**
❑ Yellow guitar
❑ Pink keyboard

Singing & dancing fun with StarSong

❑ **StarSong**
❑ Aqua mirror with ballet bar
❑ Yellow ballet bag

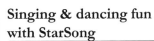

Skating fun with Scootaloo

❑ **Scootaloo**
❑ Pink water bottle
❑ Bright pink traffic cone
❑ Orange standing sign

Supermarket Store

The Supermarket Store came complete with a shopping cart, checkout counter, New Look style Pinkie Pie and lots of food accessories. Oddly, the food accessories in this set were made in very strange colors including green bread and blue bananas.

- **Pinkie Pie VIII**
- Orange display shelf
- Pink checkout counter with orange cash register
- Green and pink shopping cart
- Orange and yellow hanging scale
- Brown shopping bag
- Green loaves of bread
- Green sliced bread loaf
- Orange milk carton
- Pink cans
- Green and pink watermelon
- Yellow cake with white icing
- Green doughnuts on tray
- Yellow jars
- Blue cheese wheel
- Orange cereal box
- Pink apples
- Pink grapes
- Blue bananas
- Pink hair down wig
- Pink up-do wig

Sweetie Belle's Gumball House

This gumball machine shaped playset opened to reveal a kitchen and bedroom for New Look style Sweetie Belle. With the push of a button, the oven lit up and played the My Little Pony theme song. The interactive features on this set were powered by three AAA replaceable batteries.

- ❑ **Sweetie Belle II**
- ❑ Pink bed
- ❑ Pink seesaw with yellow base
- ❑ Pink table
- ❑ 2 pink chairs
- ❑ Pink alarm clock
- ❑ Pink toothbrush and yellow toothpaste
- ❑ Pink chef hat
- ❑ Chocolate muffins
- ❑ Green muffin tray
- ❑ Pink rolling pin
- ❑ Yellow spoon
- ❑ Dark pink bowl
- ❑ Pink cookie tray
- ❑ Pink and purple hair down wig
- ❑ Pink and purple pigtails wig

This set was also available as a bonus pack with alternate colors, extra accessories, and bonus Ponyville ponies in the New Look style.

Bonus Pack
- ❏ **Sweetie Belle II**
- ❏ **Pinkie Pie VIII**
- ❏ **Scootaloo V**
- ❏ **Toola-Roola VI**
- ❏ Yellow rolling pin
- ❏ Dark pink spoon
- ❏ Pink bowl
- ❏ Orange table
- ❏ 2 bright pink cups
- ❏ White milk carton
- ❏ Pink teapot
- ❏ Pink sugar bowl
- ❏ Pizza
- ❏ Pizza slice
- ❏ White pizza box

- ❏ Orange ice cream treat
- ❏ Yellow swirl ice cream treat
- ❏ Orange and white muffins
- ❏ Pink cake with white icing
- ❏ 2 pink teacups and saucers
- ❏ 2 croissants on green plates
- ❏ 2 pieces of cake on aqua plates
- ❏ Orange plate of cookies
- ❏ Orange and white tea cart
- ❏ Pink seesaw with dark pink base
- ❏ Yellow, pink, and orange wig
- ❏ Pink wig
- ❏ Pink and purple ponytail wig
- ❏ Pink and purple hair down wig
- ❏ Pink and purple pigtails wig

The World's Biggest Tea Party DVD

This DVD of the My Little Pony Live! show, The World's Biggest Tea Party came packaged with a release of Ponyville Pinkie Pie III.

- ❏ **Pinkie Pie III**
- ❏ DVD of *The World's Biggest Tea Party*
- ❏ Tea cart

Twirlin' Runway Styles

Containing only three accessories and a pony, this playset was very simplistic.

❑ **Rainbow Dash III**
  ❑ Multicolored hair down wig with headband
  ❑ Multicolored up-do wig
  ❑ Orange skirt

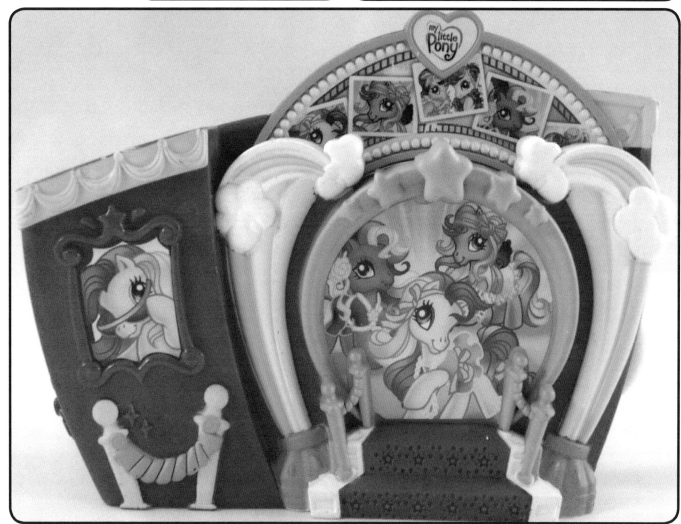

Dolly Mix Teeny Ponies

Produced and distributed by *the little factory*, a My Little Pony licensee in England, these Dolly Mixtures pony figures were 2 inches high and came with a small pink comb and candy. Each Core 7 character was packaged in a blind mix bag so the buyer would be surprised by the pony inside.

❑ **Cheerilee** (not pictured)
❑ comb
❑ **Pinkie Pie** (not pictured)
❑ comb
❑ **Rainbow Dash**
❑ comb
❑ **Scootaloo**
❑ comb
❑ **StarSong** (not pictured)
❑ comb
❑ **Sweetie Belle**
❑ comb
❑ **Toola-Roola**
❑ comb

2009 McDonald's Ponies

In 2009, McDonald's restaurants offered My Little Pony toys in their Happy Meals. This set included only six of the Core Seven ponies (Toola-Roola was not included in this set). Each pony was packaged with a special themed comb that matched their cutie mark.

❑ **Cheerilee**
❑ Green flower comb
❑ **Pinkie Pie**
❑ Blue balloon comb
❑ **Rainbow Dash**
❑ Pink rainbow comb
❑ **Scootaloo**
❑ Purple butterfly comb
❑ **StarSong**
❑ Bright pink star comb
❑ **Sweetie Belle**
❑ Light pink heart comb

So Soft Newborns

The popular baby style So Soft Ponies returned in 2009. Both were battery operated and said several phrases when you squeezed their foot including, "I'm sleepy" and "I love you, mommy!".

❏ **Cheerilee**
  ❏ Purple baby bottle

❏ **Sweetie Belle**
  ❏ Purple pacifier

So Soft Sleep and Twinkle StarSong

When you squeezed this battery operated StarSong's foot, her tummy twinkled and she spoke several phrases including, "StarSong sleepy" and ""I love you, mommy!". StarSong's eyes also closed when laid down to sleep.

❏ **StarSong**
  ❏ Pink and aqua baby bottle
  ❏ Star blanket
  ❏ Pink bowl
  ❏ Yellow spoon
  ❏ Aqua and pink pacifier

2010

Core Seven Ponies with skirts

Ponies in this set (aside from StarSong, who wore a tiara) wore skirts. Cheerilee and Pinkie Pie are identical to the 2009 New Look Core Seven Ponies release, while Rainbow Dash has a slightly darker body color than the Rainbow Dash from that set. Both StarSong and Sweetie Belle have new designs down their legs that are unique to this release. Sweetie Belle was the only pony with tinsel in her hair. Scootaloo and Toola-Roola were also sold in this assortment, but they were identical to their Twice As Fancy Ponies releases.

- ❏ **Cheerilee**
  - ❏ Green skirt
  - ❏ Dark pink brush

- ❏ **Pinkie Pie**
  - ❏ Blue skirt
  - ❏ Pink brush
- ❏ **Rainbow Dash**
  - ❏ Rainbow skirt
  - ❏ Blue brush

- ❏ **StarSong**
  - ❏ Pink tiara
- ❏ **Sweetie Belle**
  - ❏ Pink skirt

Hair Play Ponies
(reissue)

Both Cheerilee and StarSong were reissued in 2010 unchanged but packaged with a bonus special value edition Pinkie Pie. This unique version of Pinkie Pie had curly hair and extra designs all over her body.

❏ **Pinkie Pie**

Hat Box Ponies

Available exclusively at Target stores, five of the Core Seven characters came together in a special hat box set. Rainbow Dash, Scootaloo, and Sweetie Belle are all unchanged from their 2009 New Look Core Seven Ponies releases. Pinkie Pie is also identical to her Positively Pink release though StarSong's cutie mark appears on her left side which is the opposite of her 2009 New Look Core Seven version.

❏ **Pinkie Pie**
❏ **Rainbow Dash**
❏ **Scootaloo**
❏ **StarSong**
❏ **Sweetie Belle**
❏ Pink hat
❏ 2 purple bow barrettes
❏ 2 yellow flower barrettes
❏ 2 orange hearts barrettes
❏ 2 blue butterfly barrettes
❏ Yellow tiara
❏ Orange bow brush
❏ Blue comb with purple flowers

Pony and Accessory Sets

Ponies in this set came with multiple themed accessories. Pinkie Pie came with everything she needed for a sleepover while Sweetie Belle was ready to bake some confections.

- ❑ **Pinkie Pie**
  - ❑ Pajamas
  - ❑ Blue popcorn bowl
  - ❑ Pink eye mask
  - ❑ Purple radio
  - ❑ Purple bunny toy
  - ❑ Blue book
  - ❑ Pink brush

- ❑ **Sweetie Belle**
  - ❑ Purple apron
  - ❑ White chef hat
  - ❑ Pink mixing bowl with spoon
  - ❑ Pie in aqua pan
  - ❑ Cookies on pink cookie sheet
  - ❑ Purple cake
  - ❑ White icing bag

RC Rainbow Dash Plane

Packaged with a battery operated remote controlled plane that could move forward and spin, Rainbow Dash was ready to fly. This set was also sold as a bonus pack with StarSong.

- ❑ **Rainbow Dash**
  - ❑ Pink plane
- ❑ Cloud remote control
- ❑ Purple scarf

Sister's Day Out

This Newborn Cuties Family set came with a tiny infant version of Scootaloo wearing a painted outfit. Scootaloo can ride in the stroller or the baby carrier that Mom can wear.

Sister's Day Out

- ❑ **Cheerilee and Scootaloo's Mom**
- ❑ **Cheerilee**
- ❑ **Scootaloo**
- ❑ Stroller with purple seat
- ❑ Yellow and aqua baby carrier
- ❑ Pink hat
- ❑ Greenish yellow bow

Spring Pinkie Pie

While previous Spring Ponies came in sets of two or three, 2010 had only Pinkie Pie wearing bunny ears. Her packaging resembled a basket.

- ❑ **Pinkie Pie**
- ❑ Bunny ears with pink
- ❑ Yellow brush

Sweet Sounds Hairbrush

This version of Pinkie Pie came with a hairbrush big enough for you to use! This battery operated hairbrush played music and spoke with the push of a button. This Pinkie Pie has extra designs on her legs and tinsel in her hair.

- ❑ **Pinkie Pie**
- ❑ Large pink musical hairbrush
- ❑ Blue brush

Twice as Fancy Ponies

The ponies in this set are covered in artwork that includes the ponies name in the design. Each came with a brush and were often packaged with a bonus Meet The Ponies DVD. This set shares a name with a popular G1 set.

❏ **Cheerilee**
   ❏ Dark pink brush

❏ **Pinkie Pie**
   ❏ Pink brush

❏ **Rainbow Dash**
   ❏ Blue brush

❏ **Scootaloo**
   ❏ Orange brush

❏ **StarSong**
   ❏ Purple brush

❏ **Sweetie Belle**
   ❏ White brush

❑ **Toola-Roola**
   ❑ Pink brush

Valentine's Day Ponies

Both 2010 Valentine's Day Ponies have multiple designs on their bodies in addition to their regular cutie marks. Sweetie Belle has gradient shading on her legs similar to the 2008 Valentine' Day release Sweetie Belle.

❑ **Pinkie Pie**
   ❑ Pink brush

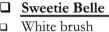

❑ **Sweetie Belle**
❑ White brush

2010 Convention Exclusive Pony

Available exclusively to attendees of the 2010 My Little Pony Conventions including the US My Little Pony Fair in Louisville, Kentucky and the UK Ponycon in Birmingham, this pony was part of the Art Pony series aimed at collectors.

❑ **2010 Convention Exclusive Pony**

2010 San Diego Comic Con Pony

In 2010, the Hasbro booth at the San Diego Comic Convention (SDCC) offered an exclusive pony to attendees. Unlike previously released Comic Con Ponies, this pony was not superhero themed. Her cutie marks resembled graffiti with the words "Pony Power" and "MLP" on her sides.

❑ **2010 SDCC Pony**

Friendship is Magic Gift Set

Hasbro released this boxed set of molded characters to promote *My Little Pony: Friendship is Magic*, an animated series that premiered on October 10, 2010 on The Hub television network in the US. The ponies in this set ranged in size from 4 to 6 inches with Princess Celestia being the largest. This set, like the show, featured characters from all three generations of My Little Pony including Spike the Dragon from the 1983 Dream Castle playset, G3 Core 7 staple Pinkie Pie and Applejack with her G1 symbol and coloring. The Princess Celestia figure, in this and most subsequent releases, is pink though her body is white in the animated series and accompanying storybook.

❏ **Princess Celestia**

❏ **Applejack**　　❏ **Pinkie Pie**　　❏ **Twilight Sparkle**　　❏ **Spike**

❏ *Friendship is Magic* storybook

Carry Bag

Containing multiple previously released Ponyville Ponies and accessories, this set came in a vinyl carrying case with a zipper. Pinkie Pie, Scootaloo, and StarSong's painted outfits appear in different colors and several accessories have alternate colors than those previously released.

- ❏ **Pinkie Pie**
- ❏ **Scootaloo**
- ❏ **StarSong**
- ❏ **Sweetie Belle**
- ❏ Pink flowers in pot
- ❏ Pink butterfly
- ❏ Pink magnifying glass
- ❏ Pink, purple, and yellow balance beam
- ❏ Pink gym bag
- ❏ Pink popcorn box
- ❏ Pink and green pinwheel
- ❏ Pink and green cotton candy
- ❏ Pink guitar
- ❏ Blue keyboard
- ❏ Vinyl heart shaped carry bag

Celebrate Spring with Cheerilee and Rainbow Dash

This spring themed Ponyville pack featured two New Look ponies, an animal friend and several fun accessories.

- ❏ **Cheerilee VI**
- ❏ **Rainbow Dash VIII**
- ❏ Pink wig
- ❏ Multicolored wig with bunny ears
- ❏ Yellow bunny
- ❏ Bouquet of orange and pink flowers
- ❏ Green skirt

Mermaid Ponies

Ponyville Ponies went under the sea in 2010 with a mermaid theme. According to their packaging, "Whenever the ponies visit the sea, they magically become beautiful mermaids!" Each Ponyville Mermaid Pony came packaged with several small beach-themed accessories. Stickers, found in all Mermaid Pony packages, could be used to complete an underwater scene.

❑ **Mermaid Pony sticker scene**

❑ **Cheerilee IX**
- ❑ Purple sandcastle
- ❑ Orange sand pail
- ❑ Yellow shovel
- ❑ Pink seal friend
- ❑ Yellow seal charm
- ❑ Seal sticker

❑ **Pinkie Pie XI**
- ❑ Orange boom box
- ❑ Yellow tropical drinks
- ❑ Purple crab friend
- ❑ Orange seahorse charm
- ❑ Seahorse sticker

❑ **Rainbow Dash XI**
- ❑ Yellow treasure chest
- ❑ Purple shell compact
- ❑ Pink hand mirror
- ❑ Pink whale friend
- ❑ Yellow whale charm
- ❑ Whale sticker

❑ **Scootaloo VIII**

- ❑ Yellow towel
- ❑ Purple surfboard
- ❑ Purple sunscreen
- ❑ Purple sunglasses
- ❑ Green turtle friend
- ❑ Orange starfish charm
- ❑ Starfish sticker

❑ **Sweetie Belle IV**

- ❑ Pink basket
- ❑ Green pitcher
- ❑ 2 pink mugs
- ❑ Purple plate of cookies
- ❑ Orange fish friend
- ❑ Purple shell charm
- ❑ Shell sticker

Mermaid Accessory Sets

Each Mermaid Accessory Set included two Ponyville Mermaid Ponies and a variety of themed accessories.

Get Pretty Beauty Set with Scootaloo and Cheerilee
- ❑ **Cheerilee X**
- ❑ **Scootaloo VII**
- ❑ Blue coral vanity with mirror and sink
- ❑ Green skirt
- ❑ Blue skirt
- ❑ Green lotion
- ❑ Green perfume
- ❑ Green bottle
- ❑ Green spray bottle
- ❑ Green shell compact
- ❑ Pink hair dryer
- ❑ 2 large pink necklaces
- ❑ 3 small pink necklaces
- ❑ Green hair brush
- ❑ Pink shell purse
- ❑ Blue sea turtle charm
- ❑ Sea turtle sticker

Teacups and Treats with Sweetie Belle and Toola-Roola
- ❑ **Sweetie Belle IV**
- ❑ **Toola-Roola VII**
- ❑ Blue and orange table
- ❑ Blue tea cart
- ❑ Purple layered cake
- ❑ Menu board
- ❑ Orange teapot
- ❑ 2 orange teacups
- ❑ Purple platter of muffins
- ❑ Purple plate with cookies
- ❑ Purple plate with cupcake
- ❑ 2 yellow star sandwiches on purple plates
- ❑ Purple bowl of ice cream
- ❑ Blue bowl with lid
- ❑ 2 pieces of cake on purple plates
- ❑ Pastry on purple plate
- ❑ 2 menus
- ❑ Orange fish charm
- ❑ Fish sticker

Mermaid Dolphin Carriage with Rainbow Dash and StarSong
- ❑ **Rainbow Dash XII**
- ❑ **StarSong V**
- ❑ Pink clam carriage
- ❑ Blue dolphin friend
- ❑ Pink coral signpost
- ❑ Purple treasure chest
- ❑ Purple hermit crab friend
- ❑ Blue fish friend
- ❑ Pink starfish friend
- ❑ Pink large jewel pile
- ❑ Purple small jewel pile
- ❑ Blue small jewel pile
- ❑ Treasure map
- ❑ Purple charm bracelet
- ❑ Purple octopus charm
- ❑ Octopus sticker

Mermaid Ponies Birthday Splash

Available exclusively at Toys R Us stores, this set included five Mermaid Ponies and party themed accessories.

- ❑ **Cheerilee X**
- ❑ **Pinkie Pie XII**
- ❑ **Rainbow Dash XII**
- ❑ **StarSong V**
- ❑ **Toola-Roola VII**
- ❑ 2 blue/white party hats
- ❑ Pink table with balloon
- ❑ Orange and pink cake
- ❑ 2 pieces of cake
- ❑ Pink boom box
- ❑ Pink punch bowl
- ❑ Yellow ladle
- ❑ 2 yellow mugs
- ❑ Red gift box
- ❑ Yellow gift box
- ❑ Orange teddy bear
- ❑ Pink starfish charm
- ❑ Starfish sticker

Mermaid Pony Castle

The Mermaid Pony Castle was the only Ponyville Playset of 2010. This sandcastle shaped set played the My Little Pony theme while the carousel rotated. The Pinkie Pie mermaid figure included was sized to ride and the set featured a variety of tropical accessories.

- **Pinkie Pie XII**
- Orange hammock
- Green basket
- Pink treasure chest
- Orange sand castle
- Pink charm bracelet
- Yellow plate of cookies
- Pink plate of cookies
- Pink tropical drink
- Yellow tropical drink
- Yellow pineapple and slice
- Pink watermelon
- Purple jewel pile
- Purple seal friend
- Purple sea turtle friend
- Green sandcastle charm
- Sandcastle sticker

Ponyville Eggs

Unlike the 2008 Ponyville Easter Egg set which contained six eggs, only two eggs were available in 2010.

- ☑ **Pinkie Pie VIII**
- ☑ **Rainbow Dash VIII**
- ☐ Pink egg
- ☐ Pink wig
- ☐ Blue egg
- ☐ Multicolored wig

Ponyville Ponies

This set of three Ponyville Ponies was available exclusively at Kohl's stores.

- ☑ **Rainbow Dash VIII**
- ☑ **Pinkie Pie VIII**
- ☑ **Scootaloo V**
- ☐ Multicolored wig
- ☐ Pink wig
- ☐ Pink and purple wig

Valentine's Day Ponyville Set

Pinkie Pie and Sweetie Belle Ponyville figures came in a tube decorated with hearts for Valentine's Day.

- ☑ **Pinkie Pie VIII**
- ☑ **Sweetie Belle II**
- ☐ Bright pink gift box
- ☐ Orange plate of cookies
- ☐ Pink and purple wig
- ☐ Pink wig

Blind Bag Ponyville Ponies

Packaged in small individual packets, these miniatures were not marked with the pony's name. It was a surprise which pony was inside the packet and a challenge to collect them all. Blind Bag Ponyville Ponies were available in parts of Europe and never saw a North American release. The cutie marks of the Blind Bag Ponyville Ponies are simplified, displaying less detail. This set contained only Core Seven characters and each pony had molded hair. Included in the set were three special translucent ponies: two different versions of Pinkie Pie and a StarSong. The collector's cards from this set are featured in the appendix.

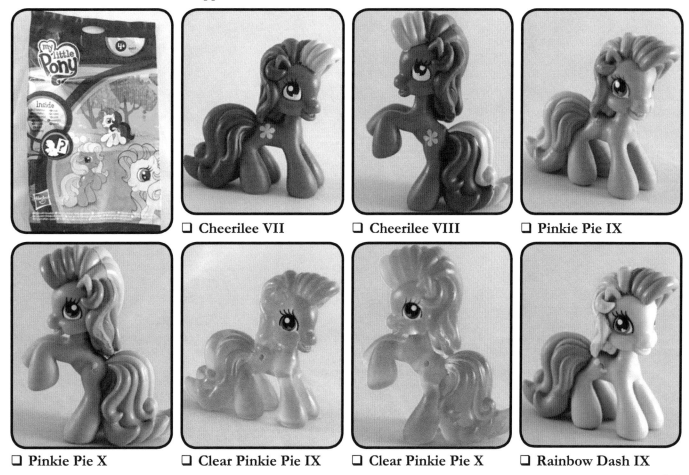

❏ Cheerilee VII   ❏ Cheerilee VIII   ❏ Pinkie Pie IX

❏ Pinkie Pie X   ❏ Clear Pinkie Pie IX   ❏ Clear Pinkie Pie X   ❏ Rainbow Dash IX

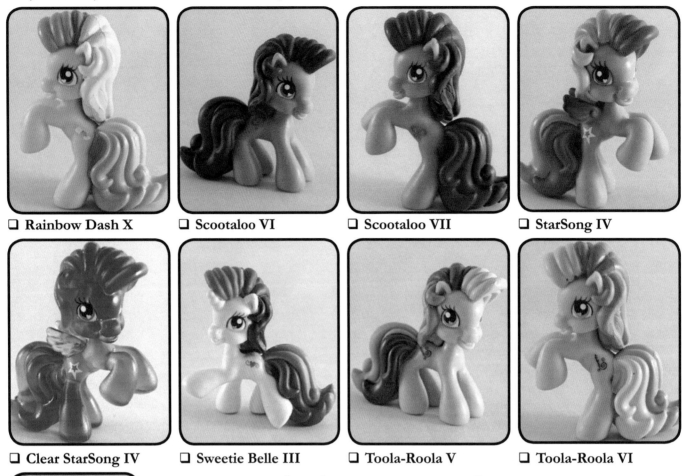

❑ **Rainbow Dash X** ❑ **Scootaloo VI** ❑ **Scootaloo VII** ❑ **StarSong IV**

❑ **Clear StarSong IV** ❑ **Sweetie Belle III** ❑ **Toola-Roola V** ❑ **Toola-Roola VI**

Blind Bag Mermaid Ponies

Packaged in small individual packets, these miniatures were not marked with the pony's name.

It was a surprise which pony was inside the packet and a challenge to collect them all. Blind Bag Mermaid Ponies were available in parts of Europe and never saw a North American release. The cutie marks of the Blind Bag Mermaid Ponies are simplified, displaying less detail. This set contained only Core Seven characters and each pony had molded hair. Each Mermaid Pony came packaged with a trading card, shell purse, and a sticker. The collector's cards from this set are featured in the appendix.

❑ **Cheerilee XI** ❑ **Clear Cheerilee XI** ❑ **Pinkie Pie XIII** ❑ **Clear Pinkie Pie XIII**

❑ Glitter Pinkie Pie XIII   ❑ Rainbow Dash XIII   ❑ Clear Rainbow Dash XIII   ❑ Glitter Rainbow Dash XIII

❑ Scootaloo IX   ❑ Clear Scootaloo IX   ❑ StarSong VI   ❑ Clear StarSong VI

❑ Glitter StarSong VI   ❑ Sweetie Belle V   ❑ Clear Sweetie Belle V

❑ Glitter Sweetie Belle V   ❑ Toola-Roola VIII   ❑ Clear Toola-Roola VIII

Dolly Mix Teeny Ponies (G1)

Produced and distributed by *the little factory* , a My Little Pony licensee in England, these Dolly Mixtures retro pony figures were 2 inches high and came packaged with a pink comb and candy. Each G1 pony character was packaged in a blind mix bag so, when opened, the buyer was surprised by the pony inside.

❑ **Applejack**
(not pictured)
❑ Pink comb
❑ **Blossom**
❑ Pink comb
❑ **Blue Belle**
❑ Pink comb
❑ **Cotton Candy**
❑ Pink comb
❑ **Cherries Jubilee**
❑ Pink comb
❑ **Glory**
❑ Pink comb
❑ **Gusty**
(not pictured)
❑ Pink comb
❑ **Firefly**
❑ Pink comb
❑ **Heart Throb**
❑ Pink comb
❑ **Lemon Drop**
❑ Pink comb
❑ **Lickety-Split**
❑ Pink comb
❑ **Mainsail**
❑ Pink comb
❑ **Medley**
❑ Pink comb
❑ **Minty**
❑ Pink comb
❑ **Powder**
❑ Pink comb
❑ **Princess Sparkle**
❑ Pink comb
❑ **Shady**
❑ Pink comb
❑ **Snuzzle**
❑ Pink comb
❑ **Sundance**
(not pictured)
❑ Pink comb
❑ **Tic-Tac-Toe**
❑ Pink comb

So Soft Newborns

Soft and huggable, Rainbow Dash was ready for bath time play, while the battery operated Pinkie Pie said several phrases including, "I'm hungry" and "La la la" when you squeezed her foot.

❏ **Rainbow Dash**
❏ Pink washcloth
❏ Yellow ducky
❏ Diaper

❏ **Pinkie Pie**
❏ Yellow and aqua baby bottle

Cheer Me Up Cheerilee

Packaged with everything needed to make Cheerilee all better, Cheerilee said a variety of phrases including, "Achoo! Is it time for my medicine?" and "Thank you for taking care of me."

❏ **Cheerilee**
❏ Pink and aqua stethoscope
❏ Yellow thermometer
❏ Purple medicine spoon

Pinkie Pie's Animated Storyteller

This huggable battery operated plush Pinkie Pie, moved her mouth as she told stories and sang songs. Packaged with four story books, the easy to use buttons on her front leg controlled this 12 inches storyteller.

- ❑ **Pinkie Pie**
- ❑ Cheerilee storybook
- ❑ Pinkie Pie storybook
- ❑ Scootaloo storybook
- ❑ Sweetie Belle storybook

New Look Style Plush

Large 18" floppy New Look style plush were available during 2010. Rainbow Dash was a Toys R Us exclusive.

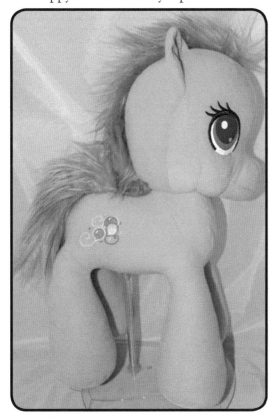

❑ **Pinkie Pie**   ❑ **Rainbow Dash**

2011

Apple Bloom and Sweetie Belle Fun at the Fair

There were plenty of prizes for Apple Bloom and Sweetie Belle to win in this set. A former member of the Core 7, Sweetie Belle was now young enough to be Rarity's little sister. Some early releases contained Scootaloo instead of Apple Bloom even though the packaging clearly read Apple Bloom. This was corrected in later releases. Neither pony in this set has a cutie mark.

- ❑ **Apple Bloom**
- ❑ **Sweetie Belle**
- ❑ Pink prize shelf
- ❑ Pink balloon
- ❑ Yellow apples
- ❑ 2 yellow ice cream cones
- ❑ Orange ice cream cone
- ❑ Orange teddy bear

Celebration at Canterlot Castle

Available exclusively at Target stores as part of their Canterlot promotion, this set included multiple accessories and a new pony, Starbeam Twinkle. Many of the accessories in this set were originally released as part of the Ponyville line.

- ❑ **Twilight Sparkle**
- ❑ **Starbeam Twinkle**
- ❑ Pink vanity
- ❑ Purple and pink table with attached pink balloon
- ❑ Pink/blue tea cart
- ❑ Yellow punch bowl with ladle
- ❑ 2 yellow mugs
- ❑ Pink ice cream sundae
- ❑ Pink cake slice
- ❑ Pink tea tray
- ❑ Purple teapot
- ❑ 2 purple teacups with saucers
- ❑ Purple creamer
- ❑ Purple sugar bowl
- ❑ 2 pink heart jewel barrettes
- ❑ 2 blue flower barrettes
- ❑ Pink gift box
- ❑ Pink cake
- ❑ Purple scepter
- ❑ Blue treasure chest
- ❑ Purple jewel comb

Fashion Style Ponies

At 8 inches tall, Fashion Style Ponies were larger than a typical pony and came with a variety of dress up accessories. This set consisted of the six main characters from *My Little Pony: Friendship is Magic*, often referred to collectively as the Mane 6. From this point forward, though originally earth ponies, Rainbow Dash and Fluttershy were now pegasus ponies while Rarity and Fluttershy each had completely new cutie marks, hair and body colors.

❑ **Applejack**
- ❑ Pink cowboy hat
- ❑ Purple saddle blanket
- ❑ Pink and brown saddle
- ❑ Brown saddle bag
- ❑ 4 pink fringe shoes
- ❑ Apples
- ❑ Purple apple rosette barrette
- ❑ Purple apple barrette
- ❑ Green apple barrette
- ❑ Dark pink flower barrette
- ❑ Pink flower barrette
- ❑ Dark pink apple comb

❑ **Fluttershy**
- ❑ Pink butterfly cape
- ❑ 4 pink shoes
- ❑ Green basket
- ❑ White bunny friend
- ❑ Purple flower barrette
- ❑ Green flower barrette
- ❑ Blue butterfly barrette
- ❑ Orange butterfly barrette
- ❑ Purple butterfly comb

❏ **Pinkie Pie**

❏ Pink / purple polka dot skirt
❏ Pink and blue saddle
❏ Pink with purple bow headband
❏ 4 transparent purple shoes
❏ Pink iced cupcakes
❏ Purple covered plate
❏ Pink wrapped candy barrette
❏ Blue wrapped candy barrette
❏ Purple ribbon barrettes
❏ Yellow ribbon barrette
❏ Blue heart balloon barrette with ribbons
❏ Blue bow brush

❏ **Rainbow Dash**

❏ Rainbow dress
❏ Pink sunglasses
❏ 4 pink winged shoes
❏ Yellow wings barrette
❏ Orange cloud barrette
❏ Purple cloud barrette
❏ Green shooting heart barrettes
❏ Pink shooting heart barrette
❏ Purple heart bracelet
❏ Orange rainbow and cloud comb

❏ **Rarity**

❏ Pink and purple fuzzy animal print saddle blanket
❏ Purple saddle bags
❏ 4 pink translucent shoes with diamonds
❏ Blue necklace
❏ Pink jewel barrette
❏ Dark pink barrette
❏ Blue heart jewel barrette
❏ Purple heart jewel barrette
❏ Blue crown barrette with ribbons
❏ Purple jewel comb

❏ **Twilight Sparkle**

❏ Pink cape with fur trim
❏ Yellow star tiara
❏ 4 yellow star shoes
❏ Yellow star barrette
❏ Pink star barrette
❏ Blue shooting star barrette
❏ Pink shooting star barrette
❏ Blue star barrette
❏ Pink star comb

Fashion Style Set

Available exclusively at Target stores as part of their Canterlot promotion, this set included Princess Celestia and Princess Luna in the larger Fashion Style and multiple accessories.

Princess Luna and Princess Celestia Fashion Style Set

- ❏ **Princess Celestia**
- ❏ **Princess Luna**
- ❏ Pink standing mirror
- ❏ Blue and purple gown
- ❏ Pink scarf
- ❏ Yellow tiara
- ❏ Blue and yellow wand
- ❏ 4 purple translucent shoes
- ❏ 2 yellow heart jewel barrettes
- ❏ 2 pink rose barrettes
- ❏ Pink butterfly clip with orange hair
- ❏ Blue jewel comb
- ❏ Purple treasure chest
- ❏ Yellow hand mirror
- ❏ Purple, pink, and gold gown
- ❏ Purple scarf
- ❏ Pink tiara
- ❏ Yellow bracelet
- ❏ 4 pink shoes
- ❏ Pink necklace
- ❏ 2pink star barrettes
- ❏ Pink butterfly clip with pink hair
- ❏ Gem stickers

Fluttershy's Nursery Tree

Fluttershy could take care of all her baby animal friends using the accessories in this set.

- ❏ **Fluttershy**
- ❏ Tree with leaf hammock
- ❏ Brown highchair
- ❏ Orange wagon
- ❏ 2 purple bunny friends
- ❏ 2 brown chipmunk friends
- ❏ Green bottle
- ❏ Lettuce
- ❏ Carrots

Glimmer Wings Ponies

Glimmer Wings Ponies each had large butterfly-like wings that you could move manually. Each came packaged with an animal friend.

❑ **Ploomette**
❑ Blue and pink peacock friend

❑ **Rainbow Dash**
❑ Yellow and pink dragonfly friend

❑ **Rarity**
  ❑ Purple butterfly friend

Pinkie Pie and Sweetie Belle's Sweets Boutique

With plenty of sweet treats, Pinkie Pie and Sweetie Belle could run their own business using this set. Sweetie Belle does not have a cutie mark.

- ❑ **Pinkie Pie**
- ❑ **Sweetie Belle**
- ❑ Pink and yellow cake stand
- ❑ Yellow counter
- ❑ Blue shopping cart
- ❑ Pink and blue gum ball machine
- ❑ Blue cash register
- ❑ Orange cake slice
- ❑ Pink popsicle
- ❑ Green and white cupcakes
- ❑ Orange milk carton
- ❑ Purple lollipop
- ❑ Yellow banana and apple

Playful Ponies

With four waves of Playful Ponies released over the course of the year, this is one of the largest sets. Every pony in this set came with an animal friend. The first wave consisted of the main cast of *My Little Pony: Friendship is Magic* and two additional characters. Daisy Dreams (packaged with Fluttershy) and Rainbow Flash (packaged with Rainbow Dash), were available as part of bonus packs outside of the United States. Though previously an earth pony, Rainbow Flash was now a unicorn.

- ❑ **Applejack**
- ❑ Brown puppy friend
- ❑ Dark pink saddle
- ❑ Yellow comb
- ❑ **Fluttershy**
- ❑ White bunny friend
- ❑ Orange wagon
- ❑ Lavender comb

- ❑ **Pinkie Pie**
- ❑ Yellow mouse friend
- ❑ Blue saddle
- ❑ Pink comb
- ❑ **Rainbow Dash**
- ❑ Brown squirrel friend
- ❑ Pink wagon
- ❑ Pinkish purple comb

❑ **Rarity**
❑ Blue bird friend
❑ Pink saddle
❑ Lavender comb
❑ **Twilight Sparkle**
❑ Pink and purple owl friend
❑ Yellow saddle
❑ Lavender comb

❑ **Daisy Dreams**
❑ Yellow and pink butterfly friend
❑ Blue saddle
❑ Yellow comb
❑ **Rainbow Flash**
❑ Green turtle friend
❑ Yellow saddle
❑ Pink comb

In addition to Applejack, Pinkie Pie, Rarity, and Twilight Sparkle, who were re-released with the same accessories as above, this second wave included Cheerilee and Lily Blossom.

❑ **Cheerilee**
❑ **Variation: Cheerilee without bangs**
❑ Yellow and red ladybug friend
❑ Lavender wagon
❑ Yellow comb
❑ **Lily Blossom**
❑ White swan friend
❑ Pink wagon
❑ Pink comb

Fluttershy, Pinkie Pie, and Twilight Sparkle were also re-released in the third wave with some familiar friends. Though originally an earth pony, Blossomforth was now a pegasus and both she and Cupcake had completely new looks including new cutie marks, hair and body colors. Cupcake was labeled "Sugar Cup" in some international releases.

❑ **Blossomforth**
❑ Pink hedgehog friend
❑ Purple wagon
❑ Yellow comb
❑ **Cupcake**
❑ White and purple raccoon friend
❑ Yellow saddle
❑ Dark pink comb

Princess Celestia

Standing ten inches high, Princess Celestia could say a variety of phrases and move her wings up and down with the push of the button located on her cutie mark. She said a variety of phrases including, "I will light the way!" "Let's fly to the Castle!" "Spectacular!" and "My barrettes look so pretty!"

- ❏ **Princess Celestia**
- ❏ Yellow crown
- ❏ Yellow necklace
- ❏ Yellow rose barrette
- ❏ Aqua rose barrette
- ❏ Purple jewel barrette
- ❏ Pink jewel barrette
- ❏ Purple comb

Princess Celestia and Princess Luna Set

Released as part of the Canterlot promotion at Target stores, Princess Celestia had molded hair and came with her sister, Princess Luna. Princess Celestia's wings are transparent in this set.

- ❏ **Princess Celestia**
- ❏ **Princess Luna**
- ❏ Yellow crown
- ❏ Yellow tiara
- ❏ Pink with gold cape
- ❏ Mint star barrette
- ❏ Dark pink comb

Rainbow Dash's Camping Trip

This set had everything Rainbow Dash needed to go camping.

- ❑ **Rainbow Dash**
- ❑ Purple tent
- ❑ Campfire
- ❑ Yellow lantern with purple handle
- ❑ Pink mug
- ❑ Purple mug
- ❑ 2 sticks with marshmallows
- ❑ White puppy friend
- ❑ Pink squirrel friend

Riding Along Ponies

Every pony in this set came with a scooter and an animal friend. Outside the US, Rainbow Dash was sold with a bonus Skywishes pony in some packages. Though originally an earth pony, Skywishes was now a pegasus.

- ❑ **Fluttershy**
- ❑ Orange scooter with aqua basket
- ❑ Aqua scarf
- ❑ Purple flowers in a pink pot
- ❑ Pink and purple butterfly friend

- ❑ **Rainbow Dash**
- ❑ Purple scooter with pink rainbow basket
- ❑ Pink visor
- ❑ Blue water bottle
- ❑ 2 pink knee pads
- ❑ Green turtle friend

❑ **Twilight Sparkle**
- ❑ Dark pink scooter
- ❑ Blue helmet
- ❑ Orange book
- ❑ Pink kitty friend

❑ **Skywishes**

Royal Ball at Canterlot Castle

The ponies (and Spike the dragon) were dressed to attend a Royal Ball in this set sold exclusively at Target stores as part of their Canterlot promotion. Ponies in this set had tinsel in their hair and came wearing tiaras and skirts or capes. The accessory colors of this set can vary.

❑ **Spike the Dragon**
- ❑ Dark pink bow tie

☐ **Applejack**
- ☐ Pink cape
- ☐ Purple tiara

☐ **Fluttershy**
- ☐ Pink metallic skirt
- ☐ Pink tiara

☐ **Pinkie Pie**
- ☐ Blue cape
- ☐ Blue tiara

☐ **Rainbow Dash**
- ☐ Purple metallic skirt
- ☐ Purple tiara

☐ **Rarity**
- ☐ Dark purple cape
- ☐ Yellow tiara

☐ **Twilight Sparkle**
- ☐ Gold metallic skirt
- ☐ Yellow tiara

Royal Friends

This set included Princess Celestia, her faithful student Twilight Sparkle and Spike the Dragon. This version of Princess Celestia had brushable hair.

☐ **Princess Celestia**
☐ **Twilight Sparkle**
☐ **Spike the Dragon**

☐ Yellow necklace
☐ Yellow tiara
☐ Yellow star tiara

Shine Bright Ponies

Pressing a button on the back a Shine Bright Pony (under the removable saddle) would activate a special light-up feature. Light up elements included Pinkie Pie's necklace, Rarity's horn and Rainbow Dash's wings.

- ❑ **Pinkie Pie II**
- ❑ Yellow, pink, and blue saddle
- ❑ Orange gift box
- ❑ **Rainbow Dash II**
- ❑ Rainbow saddle
- ❑ Yellow rosette barrette

- ❑ **Rarity II**
- ❑ Pink and purple saddle
- ❑ Purple hand mirror

A second wave of Shine Bright Ponies were available exclusively at Target stores as part of their Canterlot promotion. Pinkie Pie was released with subtle differences (including saddle color) while Fluttershy's wings lit up.

- ❑ **Fluttershy II**
- ❑ Pink, aqua, and purple saddle
- ❑ Lavender tiara
- ❑ Pink comb
- ❑ **Pinkie Pie II**
- ❑ Purple, pink, and yellow saddle
- ❑ Yellow tiara
- ❑ Purple comb

Spring Fluttershy

This special Fluttershy had flowers on her front leg in addition to her butterflies cutie mark.

- ❑ **Fluttershy**
- ❑ Lavender basket with aqua handle
- ❑ Yellow flower
- ❑ Lavender comb

Valentine's Day Pinkie Pie

This special Pinkie Pie had hearts on her front leg in addition to her familiar balloons cutie mark.

- ❑ **Pinkie Pie**
- ❑ Pink heart ring
- ❑ Sticker sheet
- ❑ Pink comb

Applejack's Farm Truck

With room for two ponies to ride, this farm truck allowed Applejack to haul everything she needed around Sweet Apple Acres. Accessory colors of the saddle, bandana, and barrettes can vary.

- ❑ **Applejack**
- ❑ Bright pink farm truck
- ❑ Blue saddle
- ❑ Pink bandana
- ❑ Yellow rope
- ❑ Blue bowl
- ❑ Apples
- ❑ Pink rosette barrette

Applejack's Sweet Apple Barn

This barn was big enough to house all the supplies Applejack needed to run the family farm.

- ❑ **Applejack**
- ❑ Barn
- ❑ Yellow farm cart
- ❑ Purple shovel
- ❑ Blue pail
- ❑ Yellow hay bale
- ❑ Purple watering can
- ❑ Yellow rope
- ❑ 2 carrots
- ❑ Apple
- ❑ White kitty friend
- ❑ White chicken friend

Canterlot Castle

Available exclusively at Target stores as part of their Canterlot promotion, this set included many accessories, Pinkie Pie and a Shine Bright version of Princess Luna with light up wings. The castle part of this set was made of thick cardboard and opened and closed to create a carrying case. Many of the accessories in this set were also released as part of the 2012 Ponyville Mermaid line and vary in color.

- **Pinkie Pie**
- **Shine Bright Princess Luna II**
- **Spike the Dragon**
- ❑ Yellow tiara
- ❑ Blue tiara
- ❑ Purple carriage
- ❑ Pink treasure chest
- ❑ Purple treasure chest
- ❑ Yellow and pink cardboard bookcase
- ❑ Pink mouse friend
- ❑ Purple large jewel cluster
- ❑ Yellow large jewel cluster
- ❑ Blue small jewel cluster
- ❑ Pink small jewel cluster
- ❑ Yellow scepter
- ❑ Blue telescope
- ❑ Pink pearl necklace
- ❑ Yellow necklace
- ❑ Blue small table
- ❑ Pink small table
- ❑ Pink tiered cake
- ❑ Blue toaster with toast
- ❑ Purple stove
- ❑ Purple frying pan with eggs
- ❑ Pink/white refrigerator
- ❑ Yellow tea cart
- ❑ Green tray
- ❑ Pink muffins
- ❑ Pink cupcakes with white icing
- ❑ Purple teapot
- ❑ Pink punch bowl with pink ladle
- ❑ 2 yellow mugs
- ❑ White milk carton
- ❑ 2 purple and white ice cream sundaes
- ❑ 2 pink plated cake slices
- ❑ Blue piano
- ❑ Pink and white vanity
- ❑ Yellow gift box
- ❑ Blue perfume bottle
- ❑ Purple pump bottle
- ❑ Yellow spray bottle
- ❑ Pink rose barrette
- ❑ Yellow jewel barrette
- ❑ Purple hearts jewel barrette
- ❑ Purple comb

Carousel Boutique

Rarity's boutique had a battery operated carousel inside that turned and played music when you slid the lever.

- ❑ **Rarity**
- ❑ **Sweetie Swirl**
- ❑ 2 tickets
- ❑ Orange drink
- ❑ Orange removable carousel pony
- ❑ Pink removable carousel pony
- ❑ Blue box of popcorn
- ❑ Orange carton of french fries
- ❑ Yellow mouse friend
- ❑ Pink saddle skirt
- ❑ Pink and purple ice cream
- ❑ Dark pink lollipop

A bonus pack of this playset with an orange colored carriage and extra animal friends was available exclusively in France.

- ❑ **Bonus Accessories**
- ❑ Orange carriage
- ❑ Orange bow barrette
- ❑ Yellow bow barrette
- ❑ Blue saddle
- ❑ Pink necklace
- ❑ Brown dog friend
- ❑ Purple squirrel friend
- ❑ Pink comb

Pinkie Pie's RC Car

Pinkie Pie's RC Car was controlled by a special battery operated remote control. The car drove forward and spun while the remote control made driving sounds.

- ❑ **Pinkie Pie**
- ❑ Pink car
- ❑ Orange and pink remote control

Ponyville Schoolhouse

Cheerilee was ready to teach the younger ponies using a variety of school themed accessories.

- ❑ **Cheerilee**
- ❑ Orange school building
- ❑ Purple swing
- ❑ Blue teacher's desk
- ❑ 2 purple student desks
- ❑ Pink pile of books
- ❑ Blue pile of books
- ❑ Purple reading glasses
- ❑ Apples
- ❑ Brown chipmunk friend
- ❑ Light pink bunny friend

Royal Gem Carriage

Rarity's royal carriage was a recolor of the carriage from the Carousel Boutique bonus set. The portrait could spin to reveal two different looks for Rarity. Accessory colors of this set can vary.

- ❏ **Rarity**
- ❏ Pink carriage
- ❏ Pink ribbon barrette
- ❏ Blue ribbon barrette
- ❏ Purple rosette barrette
- ❏ Pink ring
- ❏ Purple comb

In parts of Europe and Australia, this set came with a bonus pony, Star Swirl. Star Swirl had a whole new look with a darker hair and body color and a more symmetrical cutie mark.

- ❏ **Star Swirl**

Twilight Sparkle's Twinkling Balloon

Press the button on the side and this battery powered hot air balloon lit up and played the *My Little Pony: Friendship is Magic* theme song. There were two different variations of the Twinkling Balloon. Later releases of this set had pink decorative swirls painted on the balloon, while earlier released versions did not. In addition, the balloon skirt and ropes of both versions could appear in either pink or yellow. To make this set even more confusing for collectors, both Twinkling Balloon versions could be packaged with a Twilight Sparkle with or without bangs.

- ❑ **Twilight Sparkle**
- ❑ **Variation: Twilight Sparkle (without bangs)**
- ❑ **Spike the Dragon**

- ❑ Purple hot air balloon
- ❑ **Variation:** Purple hot air balloon with swirls
- ❑ Orange telescope

Blind Bag Miniature Ponies
(first set)

Packaged in small individual packets, these miniature ponies were not marked with the pony's name. It was a surprise which pony was inside the packet and a challenge to collect them all. However, collectors realized that a one to two digit number system code printed on the bag corresponded to the pony inside the bag. Hasbro re-released the set with a new numbering system that utilized a five digit number code but the new numbering system could be easily decoded by ignoring the first, third, and fifth numbers in the five digit code. For example, a Blind Bag Miniature Pony packet printed with the number 21765 would correspond to the pony who is number 16 of the set. The first set of Blind Bag Miniature Ponies came in pink Canterlot bags. The collector's cards from this set are featured in the appendix.

- ❑ **Pinkie Pie (01)**
- ❑ **Applejack (02)**
- ❑ **Rainbow Dash (03)**
- ❑ **Rarity (04)**

❑ **Twilight Sparkle (05)**   ❑ **Fluttershy (06)**   ❑ **Sugar Grape (07)**   ❑ **Lily Blossom (08)**

❑ **Minty (09)**   ❑ **Bumblesweet (10)**   ❑ **Fizzy Pop (11)**   ❑ **Flower Wishes (12)**

❑ **Rose Luck (13)**   ❑ **Sweetie Blue (14)**   ❑ **Pepperdance (15)**   ❑ **Lemon Hearts (16)**

❑ **Cherry Spices (17)**   ❑ **Sweetie Swirl (18)**   ❑ **Lucky Swirl (19)**   ❑ **Sweetcream Scoops (20)**

❏ **Firecracker Burst (21)**

❏ **Glitter Pinkie Pie (22)**

❏ **Glitter Twilight Sparkle (23)**

❏ **Glitter Rainbow Dash (24)**

Blind Bag Miniature Ponies
(second set)

The second set of Blind Bag Miniature Ponies came in purple Ponyville bags. This set was only found in Europe. This second set had the same 5 digit numbering convention as the first. The collector's cards from this set are featured in the appendix.

❏ **Pinkie Pie (01)**

❏ **Applejack (02)**

❏ **Rainbow Dash (03)**

❏ **Rarity (04)**

❏ **Twilight Sparkle (05)**

❏ **Fluttershy (06)**

❏ **Feathermay (07)**

❏ **Blossomforth (08)**

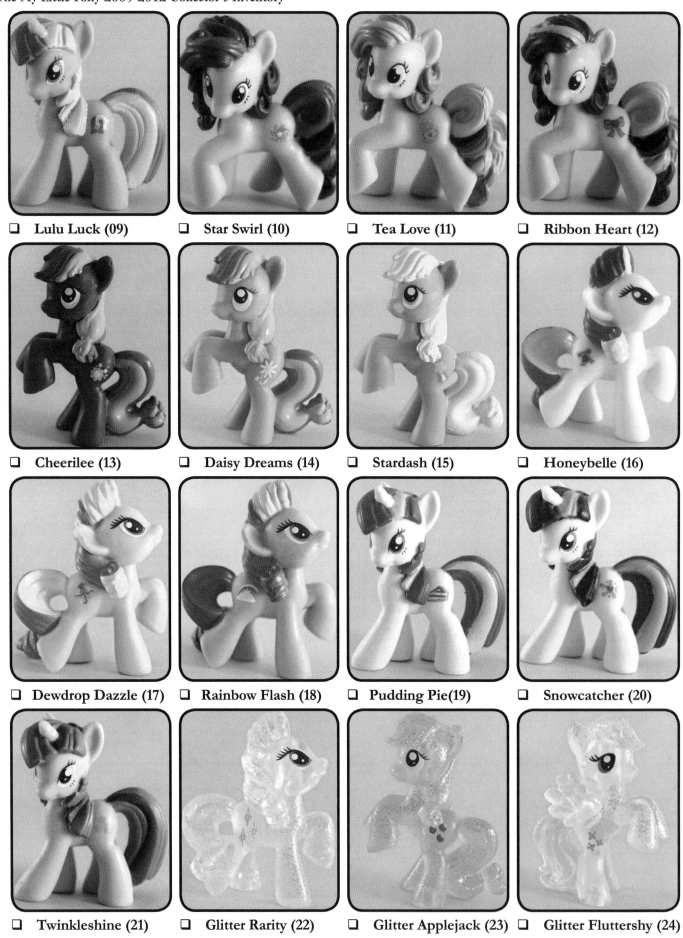

❑ **Lulu Luck (09)**   ❑ **Star Swirl (10)**   ❑ **Tea Love (11)**   ❑ **Ribbon Heart (12)**

❑ **Cheerilee (13)**   ❑ **Daisy Dreams (14)**   ❑ **Stardash (15)**   ❑ **Honeybelle (16)**

❑ **Dewdrop Dazzle (17)**   ❑ **Rainbow Flash (18)**   ❑ **Pudding Pie(19)**   ❑ **Snowcatcher (20)**

❑ **Twinkleshine (21)**   ❑ **Glitter Rarity (22)**   ❑ **Glitter Applejack (23)**   ❑ **Glitter Fluttershy (24)**

Advent Calendar

Replacing the annual Ponyville Advent Calendar, this set contained 24 doors that opened, each revealing a secret surprise.

- ❑ **Pinkie Pie**
- ❑ **Rainbow Dash**
- ❑ **Twilight Sparkle**
- ❑ 2 green picture frames
- ❑ Blue picture frame
- ❑ Brown squirrel friend
- ❑ White mouse friend
- ❑ Blue owl friend
- ❑ Purple plate of muffins
- ❑ Purple plate of cookies
- ❑ Pink slice of cake on a green plate
- ❑ Blue cake with white icing

- ❑ Purple / yellow sundae
- ❑ 2 white milk cartons
- ❑ Pink table
- ❑ White teapot
- ❑ White sugar bowl
- ❑ 3 purple teacups with saucers
- ❑ Green book
- ❑ Santa hat
- ❑ 4 white shoes
- ❑ Red gift box
- ❑ Brown mailing package
- ❑ 6 letters
- ❑ Sticker sheet

Miniature 4-Pack

Packaged together in a 4-pack, these miniature ponies are identical to those released as Miniature Singles and in the Blind Bags.

- ❑ **Pinkie Pie**
- ❑ **Rarity**
- ❑ **Rainbow Dash**
- ❑ **Twilight Sparkle**

Miniature Singles

Containing a single Miniature Pony figure on a bubble card, the ponies available in this set are identical to those released in the Miniature 4-pack and in the Blind Bags.

- ❏ **Twilight Sparkle**
- ❏ **Applejack**
- ❏ **Fluttershy**
- ❏ **Pinkie Pie**
- ❏ **Rainbow Dash**
- ❏ **Rarity**

Pony Collection Set

Available exclusively at Toys R Us stores, this set included the Mane 6 ponies from *My Little Pony: Friendship is Magic,* all of which were indentical to their Blind Bag releases, as well as six additional ponies. Though previously earth ponies, Beachberry and Gardinia Glow were now unicorns while Peachy Pie, Skywishes and Sweetsong were now pegasus ponies. Also included in this set were twelve collector cards, each showcasing a different pony included in the set. The collector's cards from this set are featured in the appendix.

❏ **Applejack**   ❏ **Fluttershy**   ❏ **Pinkie Pie**   ❏ **Rarity**

❏ **Rainbow Dash**   ❏ **Twilight Sparkle**   ❏ **Beachberry**   ❏ **Coconut Cream**

❑ **Gardinia Glow**   ❑ **Peachy Pie**   ❑ **Skywishes**   ❑ **Sweetsong**

2011 McDonald's Ponies

In 2011, McDonald's restaurants offered My Little Pony toys in their Happy Meals. This set included eight ponies that appeared in *My Little Pony: Friendship is Magic*. Each pony was packaged with a special themed comb that matched their cutie mark.

- ❏ **Applejack**
- ❏ Apple comb
- ❏ **Cheerilee**
- ❏ Flower comb
- ❏ **Fluttershy**
- ❏ Butterfly comb
- ❏ **Pinkie Pie**
- ❏ Balloon comb
- ❏ **Princess Celestia**
- ❏ Sun comb
- ❏ **Rainbow Dash**
- ❏ Lightning bolt comb
- ❏ **Rarity** (not pictured)
- ❏ Diamond comb
- ❏ **Twilight Sparkle**
- ❏ Star comb

Available exclusively at McDonald's restaurants in Brazil, this set consisted of four translucent ponies. A button on the pony made them light up.

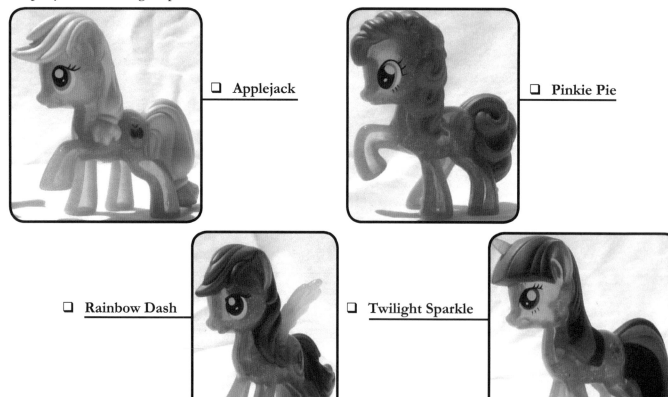

❏ **Applejack**

❏ **Pinkie Pie**

❏ **Rainbow Dash**

❏ **Twilight Sparkle**

So Soft Newborns

Soft and huggable, these So Soft ponies came packaged with accessories that allowed you to take care of them. Both Sweetie Belle and Sunny Daze were battery operated and said several phrases when you squeezed their foot including their names, "La la la" or "I have wings!" Sunny Daze's body color changed from white to purple in this release.

❑ **Sweetie Belle**
❑ Yellow and lavender baby bottle
❑ **Sunny Daze**
❑ Orange pacifier

So Soft Pinkie Pie Learns to Walk

This little Pinkie Pie walks when you hold her hands. In addition to being mobile with your help, this battery operated So Soft Pony giggled and said a variety of phrases including, "I can walk!" and "Hold my hands."

❑ **Pinkie Pie**
❑ Purple pacifier
❑ Pink food dish
❑ Purple spoon
❑ Blue bib
❑ Yellow and aqua baby bottle

Animated Storytellers

These huggable plush versions of Pinkie Pie and Twilight Sparkle, moved their mouths as they told stories and sang songs. Packaged with four story books, each pony was controlled by several buttons on their front legs. Each battery operated pony measured 12 inches high. Twilight Sparkle was available exclusively at Target stores as part of their Canterlot collection.

❑ **Pinkie Pie**

❑ *Dragonslayer* storybook

❑ *Griffon the Brush Off* storybook

❑ *Fall Weather Friends* storybook

❑ *Swarm of the Century* storybook

❑ **Twilight Sparkle**

❑ *Applebuck Season* storybook

❑ *Welcome to Ponyville* storybook

❑ *The Ticket Master* storybook

❑ *The Magic of Friendship* storybook

Plush Ponies

Two large 18" floppy plush versions of Pinkie Pie and Twilight Sparkle were available in stores during 2011. Twilight Sparkle was available exclusively at Target stores as part of their Canterlot collection, while Pinkie Pie was widely available.

 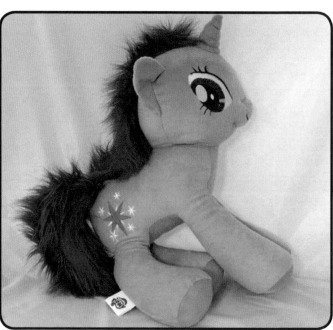

❑ **Pinkie Pie**

❑ **Twilight Sparkle**

2012

Bridle Friends

To celebrate the wedding of Princess Cadance and Shining Armor, Twilight Sparkle and the other bridesmaids came packaged with wedding themed accessories.

❏ Fluttershy
- ❏ Green piano
- ❏ Pink gift box
- ❏ Yellow flower bouquet with card
- ❏ 2 aqua rose barrettes
- ❏ Pink rose barrette
- ❏ Pink and white bridesmaid bouquet with green ribbon
- ❏ Pink necklace
- ❏ Pink skirt
- ❏ Yellow comb

❏ Pinkie Pie
- ❏ Blue and yellow tea cart
- ❏ Pink cake
- ❏ 2 pink heart jewel barrettes
- ❏ Blue heart jewel barrette
- ❏ Pink and white bridesmaid bouquet with yellow ribbon
- ❏ Pink necklace
- ❏ Yellow dress
- ❏ Blue comb

❏ Rarity
- ❏ Pink vanity
- ❏ Blue treasure chest
- ❏ Purple crown barrette with ribbons
- ❏ Blue jewel barrette
- ❏ Pink jewel barrette
- ❏ Pink and white bridesmaid bouquet with blue ribbon
- ❏ Pink necklace
- ❏ Blue skirt
- ❏ Pink comb

❏ Twilight Sparkle
- ❏ Aqua treasure chest on pink stand
- ❏ Orange book
- ❏ 2 purple star barrettes
- ❏ Pink shooting star barrette
- ❏ Pink and white bridesmaid bouquet with pink ribbon
- ❏ Pink necklace
- ❏ Pink metallic skirt
- ❏ Pink comb

Crystal Princess Ponies Collection

This set was available exclusively at Target stores as part of their Crystal Empire line.

- ❏ **Princess Luna III**
- ❏ **Princess Celestia**
- ❏ **Princess Cadance**
- ❏ Blue skirt
- ❏ Pink skirt
- ❏ Yellow skirt
- ❏ Blue tiara
- ❏ Yellow tiara
- ❏ Pink tiara
- ❏ 2 yellow flower barrettes
- ❏ 2 pink jewel barrettes
- ❏ 2 blue jewel barrettes
- ❏ Purple treasure chest
- ❏ Pink ring
- ❏ Yellow comb

Favorite Friends

Available exclusively at Toys R Us stores as part of their Collector's Series, this set included fan favorite ponies from *My Little Pony: Friendship is Magic* with glittery symbols. It also marked the first time a villain character, Nightmare Moon, appeared as a toy figure in the history of My Little Pony.

❑ **DJ Pon-3**   ❑ **Flower Wishes**   ❑ **Lemony Gem**

❑ **Nightmare Moon**   ❑ **Pinkie Pie**   ❑ **Rainbow Dash**

❑ **Trixie Lunamoon**

Fashion Style Ponies
(second set)

Designed to be dressed up and styled with accessories, the Fashion Style Ponies stood 6 inches high and were taller than typical My Little Ponies. This set consisted of Princess Celestia and Princess Luna. Unlike the previous 2011 Target exclusive Fashion Style Set release, they do not have glitter on their horns and wings.

❑ **Princess Celestia**
❑ Aqua dress with pink metallic trim
❑ Pink tiara
❑ 4 pink shoes
❑ Aqua jeweled heart barrette
❑ Purple jeweled heart barrette
❑ Pink jewel barrette
❑ Yellow jewel barrette
❑ Aqua jewel comb

❑ **Princess Luna**
❑ Blue dress with pink metallic trim
❑ Yellow tiara
❑ 4 yellow shoes
❑ Pink shooting star barrette
❑ Blue shooting star barrette
❑ Dark pink star barrette
❑ Yellow star barrette
❑ Star comb

117

Fashion Style Set
(second set)

Exclusively available at Target stores as part of their Crystal Empire line, this set featured both Princess Cadance and Shining Armor in Fashion Style with multiple accessories.

- ❑ **Princess Cadance II**
- ❑ **Shining Armor**
- ❑ White dress with metallic gold trim
- ❑ Red uniform shirt with yellow accents
- ❑ 4 transparent yellow shoes
- ❑ Purple large gift box
- ❑ Pink small gift box
- ❑ Blue crown barrette with ribbons
- ❑ Pink and purple flower bouquet
- ❑ 2 purple rings
- ❑ White jeweled heart barrette
- ❑ Pink jeweled heart barrette
- ❑ Gold tiara
- ❑ Aqua treasure chest on pink stand

Glimmer Wing Ponies
(second set)

With large wings that could be moved manually, the Glimmer Wings Ponies each came packaged with an animal friend.

❑ **Daisy Dreams**
❑ Purple butterfly friend

❑ **Fluttershy**
❑ Pink butterfly friend with yellow wings

Glimmer Wings Sets

Part of the Target exclusive Crystal Empire line, each Glimmer Wings set had one Glimmer Wings Pony along with another pony with tinsel in their hair.

❑ **Diamond Rose**
❑ **Pinkie Pie**
❑ Blue comb

❑ **Sweetsong**
❑ **Fluttershy**
❑ Pink comb

Pony School Pals

This set featured the Cutie Mark Crusaders (Apple Bloom, Scootaloo, and Sweetie Belle) along with their teacher, Miss Cheerilee. The three junior ponies have no cutie marks, a plot point in the *My Little Pony: Friendship is Magic* animated series.

❑ **Cheerilee**   ❑ **Scootaloo**
❑ **Apple Bloom**   ❑ **Sweetie Belle**

Pony Scooter Friends

Packaged as an exclusive two pack at Toys R Us stores, this set was part of their "Pony Friends Forever" (or P.F.F.) line. Accompanied with scooters, these ponies were ready to ride.

❑ **Daisy Dreams**
❑ **Rarity**
❑ Pink scooter
❑ Blue scarf
❑ Pink flowers
❑ Sticker sheet
❑ Orange scooter
❑ Aqua helmet
❑ Purple book
❑ *Friendship is Magic* story book

Princess Cadance

Princess Cadance married Twilight Sparkle's brother, Shining Armor, in the Royal Wedding episode of *My Little Pony: Friendship is Magic* and here she is in her wedding gown. With the push of the button located on her cutie mark, her wings would light up and move up and down. Princess Cadance hummed the "Wedding March" and said a variety of phrases, including "Today is my wedding day," "My dress is so pretty," and "Let's dance!".

- ❏ **Princess Cadance**
  - ❏ White wedding dress
  - ❏ Gold tiara
  - ❏ Gold comb

Princess Celestia

Available exclusively at Toys R Us stores as part of their Collector Series, this battery operated version of Princess Celestia had a white body matching her character in *My Little Pony: Friendship is Magic*. With the push of the button located on her cutie mark, her wings would light up and move up and down while she talked. She said a variety of phrases including: "I will light the way!" "Let's fly to the Castle!" "Spectacular!" and "My barrettes look so pretty!".

- ❏ **Princess Celestia**
  - ❏ Gold trimmed yellow crown
  - ❏ Gold trimmed yellow necklace
  - ❏ Purple flower barrette
  - ❏ Dark aqua jewel barrette
  - ❏ Yellow jewel barrette
  - ❏ Pink flower barrette
  - ❏ Purple comb

Princess Celestia and Friends Tea Time

Packaged as an exclusive three pack at Toys R Us stores, this set was part of their "Pony Friends Forever" (or P.F.F.) line. It included Princess Celestia, Pinkie Pie, and Rainbow Dash and everything you needed to hold a successful pony-sized tea party.

- ☑ **Princess Celestia**
- ☑ **Pinkie Pie**
- ☑ **Rainbow Dash**
- ☐ Purple table
- ☐ White tray

- ☐ Pink teapot
- ☐ Muffins
- ☐ Yellow tiara
- ☐ 3 white teacups
- ☐ 2 white cookie plates with pink cookies

- ☐ White cookie plate with purple cookie
- ☐ White pitcher
- ☐ Pink sugar bowl
- ☐ Aqua and purple tea cart
- ☐ White hat with pink ribbon
- ☐ White hat with aqua ribbon

2012 Special Edition Pony

This popular background character from *My Little Pony: Friendship is Magic* was unique because of her askew eyes. Available at both the San Diego Comic Con (SDCC) and the My Little Pony Fair, this pony was in high demand and quantities quickly sold out at both events. Limited quantities were also added to Hasbro's website, Hasbro Toyshop, but sold out in minutes. While this pony is sometimes called "Derpy" or "Ditzy Doo" by fans of the show, Hasbro never gave her an official name.

❑ **2012 Special Edition Pony**

Traveling Ponies

Traveling on the Friendship Express Train was a popular activity in 2012 and ponies in this set had everything they needed for the journey. In parts of Europe, New Zealand, and Australia, Applejack was offered as part of a bonus package with Lily Blossom and Pinkie Pie was offered with a bonus Dewdrop Dazzle both of whom were from the 2011 Playful Ponies set.

❑ **Applejack**
- ❑ Purple ladybug friend
- ❑ Pink suitcase
- ❑ 2 cardboard tickets
- ❑ Sticker sheet

❑ **Fluttershy**
- ❑ Tan chipmunk friends with purple stripes
- ❑ Aqua suitcase
- ❑ 2 cardboard tickets
- ❑ Sticker sheet

❑ **Pinkie Pie**
- ❑ Pink hedgehog friend
- ❑ Yellow suitcase
- ❑ 2 cardboard tickets
- ❑ Sticker sheet

❑ **Rainbow Dash**
- ❑ White duck friend
- ❑ Pink suitcase
- ❑ 2 cardboard tickets
- ❑ Sticker sheet

❑ **Rarity**
- ❑ Purple butterfly friend
- ❑ Blue suitcase
- ❑ 2 cardboard tickets
- ❑ Sticker sheet

❑ **Twilight Sparkle**
- ❑ White puppy friend with pink ears
- ❑ Purple suitcase
- ❑ 2 cardboard tickets
- ❑ Sticker sheet

A second wave of Traveling Ponies arrived later this same year with two new ponies. Applejack, Pinkie Pie, Rainbow Dash, and Twilight Sparkle returned unchanged from the first set. Ponies in this set were often packaged with a DVD of the *My Little Pony: Friendship Is Magic* episode, "Applebuck Season."

- ❑ **Cherry Pie**
  - ❑ White mouse friend
  - ❑ Orange suitcase
  - ❑ Sticker sheet
  - ❑ 2 tickets
- ❑ **Diamond Rose**
  - ❑ Pink swan friend
  - ❑ Pink suitcase
  - ❑ Sticker sheet
  - ❑ 2 tickets

Wedding Ponies

Everypony in this set was invited to attend the royal wedding of Princess Cadance and Twilight Sparkle's brother, Shining Armor. Each came packaged with a wedding invitation and wedding themed accessories. In the US, ponies in this set were sometimes packaged with the *My Little Pony: Friendship Is Magic* episode, "The Ticket Master."

- ❑ **Applejack**
  - ❑ Pink punch bowl and yellow ladle
  - ❑ 2 pink cups
  - ❑ Wedding invitation
  - ❑ Pink comb
- ❑ **Fluttershy**
  - ❑ Pink gift box
  - ❑ Wedding invitation
  - ❑ Pink comb

❑ **Pinkie Pie**
❑ Purple cake
❑ Wedding invitation
❑ Bright pink comb
❑ **Rainbow Dash**
❑ Aqua framed picture
❑ Wedding invitation
❑ Pink comb

❑ **Rarity**
❑ Pink purse
❑ Wedding invitation
❑ Blue comb
❑ **Twilight Sparkle**
❑ Red flower bouquet with card
❑ Wedding invitation
❑ Purple comb

A second wave of Wedding Ponies arrived later this same year with four new characters including Lyra Heartstrings and Trixie Lunamoon. In the US, this set was sometimes packaged with the *My Little Pony: Friendship Is Magic* episode, "Lesson Zero."

❑ **Cherry Berry**
❑ Pink cake
❑ Wedding invitation
❑ Yellow comb
❑ **Lyra Heartstrings**
❑ Yellow framed picture
❑ Wedding invitation
❑ Pink comb

❑ **Trixie Lunamoon**
❑ Pink gift box
❑ Wedding invitation
❑ Pink comb
❑ **Sunny Rays**
❑ Blue punch bowl
❑ Purple ladle
❑ 2 blue cups
❑ Wedding invitation
❑ Blue comb

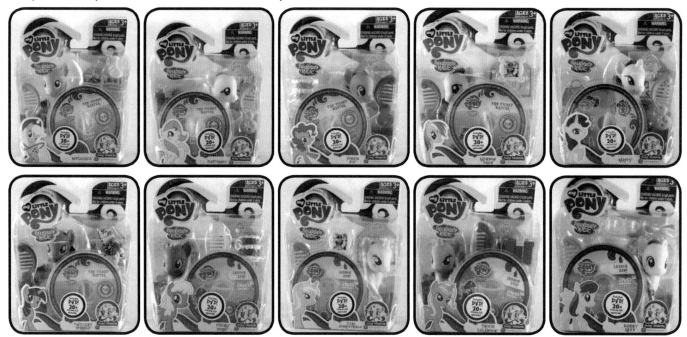

Wedding Flower Fillies

The Cutie Mark Crusaders (Apple Bloom, Scootaloo, and Sweetie Belle) served as flower girls for the wedding of Princess Cadance and Shining Armor. All three are without cutie marks.

❏ **Apple Bloom**   ❏ **Scootaloo**   ❏ **Sweetie Belle**

- ❏ White dress
- ❏ Purple dress
- ❏ Pink dress
- ❏ White flower headband
- ❏ Purple flower headband
- ❏ Pink flower headband
- ❏ White bouquet
- ❏ Purple bouquet
- ❏ Pink bouquet

Zecora

Packaged in a special box as part of the Collector's Series sold exclusively at Toys R Us, Zecora glowed in the dark.

❏ **Zecora**

Afternoon Picnic

Cherrilee and some of her favorite animal friends had everything they needed to enjoy an outdoor picnic with this set. Accessory colors can vary.

❏ **Cheerilee**
❏ Orange picnic table
❏ Aqua umbrella
❏ Purple animal friend high chair
❏ Green wagon
❏ Pink basket
❏ Pink saddle
❏ Yellow banana and apple
❏ Carrots
❏ Lettuce
❏ Yellow squirrel friend
❏ Brown bunny friend
❏ Pink baby bunny friend

Sweet Slumbers

In this set, Applejack joined Star Dreams for a slumber party that included pizza, popcorn, and watching TV. Star Dreams does not have a cutie mark.

- ❑ **Applejack**
- ❑ **Star Dreams**
- ❑ Pink and purple bed
- ❑ Pink apple-shaped television
- ❑ White pizza box
- ❑ Pizza
- ❑ Pizza slice
- ❑ Blue bowl of popcorn
- ❑ Blue teddy bear
- ❑ 4 pink slippers
- ❑ 4 smaller purple fillyslippers

Factory Error Ponies

While not meant to be available to the public, several batches of manufacturing errors have found their way online and sold to collectors. These ponies are the result of factory errors during production. Errors can include major differences such as incorrect hair color, incorrect body color, or incorrect cutie mark as well as minor differences including eye color or wrong pony head/body combinations. While the possibilities are infinite, there have been a few stand-out error ponies that have become especially popular among the collecting community.

❏ **Fashion Style Celestia with white body**

❏ **Fashion Style Rainbow Dash without wings**

❏ **Fashion Style Rarity with Princess Celestia's eyes design and hair color**

❏ **Blue Fluttershy unicorn with Rarity's eye design and blue and white hair**

❏ **Sunny Rays unicorn with aqua body, Rarity's eye design and aqua and white hair**

❏ **Pinkie Pie with bright pink body and yellow hair**

Friendship Express Train

All Aboard! Featured on *My Little Pony: Friendship is Magic*, the Friendship Express could speed ponies from Ponyville to Canterlot, the home of Princess Celestia. Packaged with Pinkie Pie, this motorized train had seven pieces of railroad track that snapped together.

- ❑ **Pinkie Pie**
- ❑ Pink train engine
- ❑ Aqua railroad cart
- ❑ 7 pieces of purple railroad track

Friendship Express Train Around Town

Available exclusively at Toys R Us stores as part of their Pony Friends Forever (P.F.F.) line, this set contained a battery operated train engine, two additional train cars, ten pieces of railroad track that snapped together, three ponies and a host of accessories. Apple Bloom does not have a cutie mark.

- ❑ **Rainbow Dash**
- ❑ **Twilight Sparkle**
- ❑ **Apple Bloom**

- ❑ Pink train engine
- ❑ Aqua train car
- ❑ Yellow ice cream train car
- ❑ 10 pieces of purple railroad track

- ❏ Purple squirrel friend
- ❏ Yellow kitty friend
- ❏ Blue bunny friend
- ❏ White chipmunk friend
- ❏ Yellow pony-shaped ice cream treat
- ❏ Orange ice cream treat
- ❏ Purple ice cream treat

- ❏ Purple ice cream scoop
- ❏ Purple basket
- ❏ Pink purse
- ❏ Pink suitcase
- ❏ Tree with red hammock
- ❏ Pop-up cardboard train station
- ❏ 3 cardboard tickets
- ❏ Map

Fluttershy's Nursery Train Car

Fluttershy was ready to ride the rails in her own car that attached to the Friendship Express Train.

- ❏ **Fluttershy**
- ❏ Purple train car
- ❏ Pink bunny friend
- ❏ 2 cardboard tickets
- ❏ Map
- ❏ Pink basket
- ❏ Orange purse

Sweetie Belle's Ice Cream Train Car

Sweetie Belle's ice cream shaped train car attached to the Friendship Express Train and included ice cream treats to share with her friends. She does not have a cutie mark.

- ❑ **Sweetie Belle**
- ❑ Orange ice cream train car
- ❑ Purple squirrel friend
- ❑ 2 cardboard tickets
- ❑ Map
- ❑ Purple pony-shaped ice cream treat
- ❑ Pink ice cream treat
- ❑ Blue ice cream treat
- ❑ Yellow ice cream scoop

Wedding Castle

The largest Friendship is Magic inspired playset to date, the Pony Princess Wedding Castle provided a fairy tale atmosphere for the royal wedding of Princess Cadance and Shining Armor.

- ❑ **Princess Cadance**
- ❑ **Shining Armor II**
- ❑ Pink butterfly friend
- ❑ Purple porch swing
- ❑ Pink wedding cake
- ❑ Gold teapot
- ❑ 2 gold teacups
- ❑ Blue table

- ❑ Purple bouquet
- ❑ Purple piano
- ❑ Pink purse
- ❑ Groom's tuxedo
- ❑ Groom's gold crown
- ❑ Wedding dress
- ❑ Wedding veil
- ❑ 2 gold rings

- ❑ Bride's gold crown
- ❑ Gold necklace
- ❑ Gold chandelier
- ❑ Gold comb

Wedding RC Car

Being the sister of the groom had its perks. Twilight Sparkle had her own battery operated radio controlled car in honor of the Royal Wedding.

- ❏ **Twilight Sparkle**
- ❏ White car
- ❏ Purple remote control

Blind Bag Miniature Ponies
(third set)

The third set of Blind Bag Miniature Ponies came in purple travel themed bags with Twilight Sparkle on the front and a small suitcase icon. Three special glow in the dark ponies were also included in this set. Lyra Heartstrings is listed as just Heartstrings in this set. The collector's cards from this set are featured in the appendix.

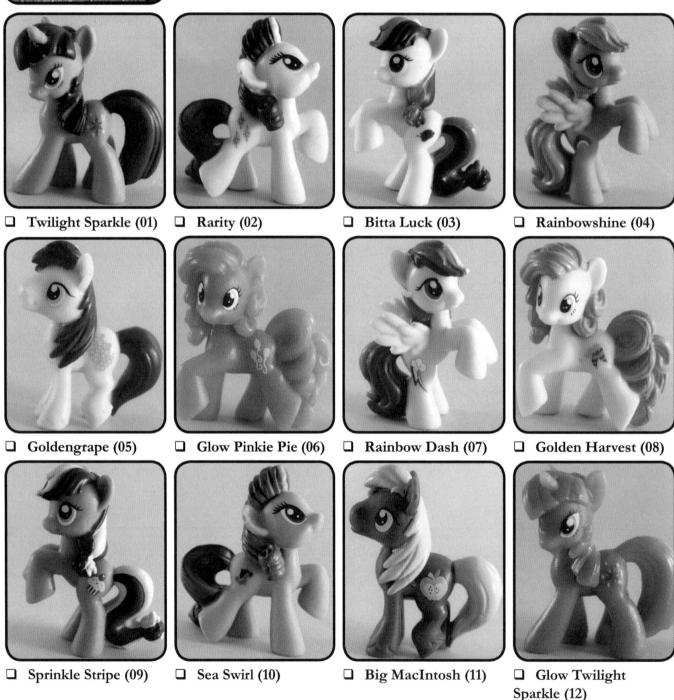

❑ **Twilight Sparkle (01)**   ❑ **Rarity (02)**   ❑ **Bitta Luck (03)**   ❑ **Rainbowshine (04)**

❑ **Goldengrape (05)**   ❑ **Glow Pinkie Pie (06)**   ❑ **Rainbow Dash (07)**   ❑ **Golden Harvest (08)**

❑ **Sprinkle Stripe (09)**   ❑ **Sea Swirl (10)**   ❑ **Big MacIntosh (11)**   ❑ **Glow Twilight Sparkle (12)**

❏ Pinkie Pie (13)   ❏ Apple Dazzle (14)   ❏ Lovestruck (15)   ❏ Berryshine (16)

❏ Meadow Song (17)   ❏ Glow Rarity (18)   ❏ Applejack (19)   ❏ Fluttershy (20)

❏ Cherry Berry (21)   ❏ Heartstrings (22)   ❏ Noteworthy (23)   ❏ Lucky Dreams (24)

Blind Bag Miniature Ponies
(fourth set)

The fourth set of Blind Bag Miniature Ponies came in blue themed bags with Rarity on the front and a small diamond icon. The miniature ponies in this set were glittery except for three special metallic ponies (Rarity, Applejack, and Pinkie Pie.) Trixie Lunamoon is listed as just Lunamoon in this set. The collector's cards from this set are featured in the appendix.

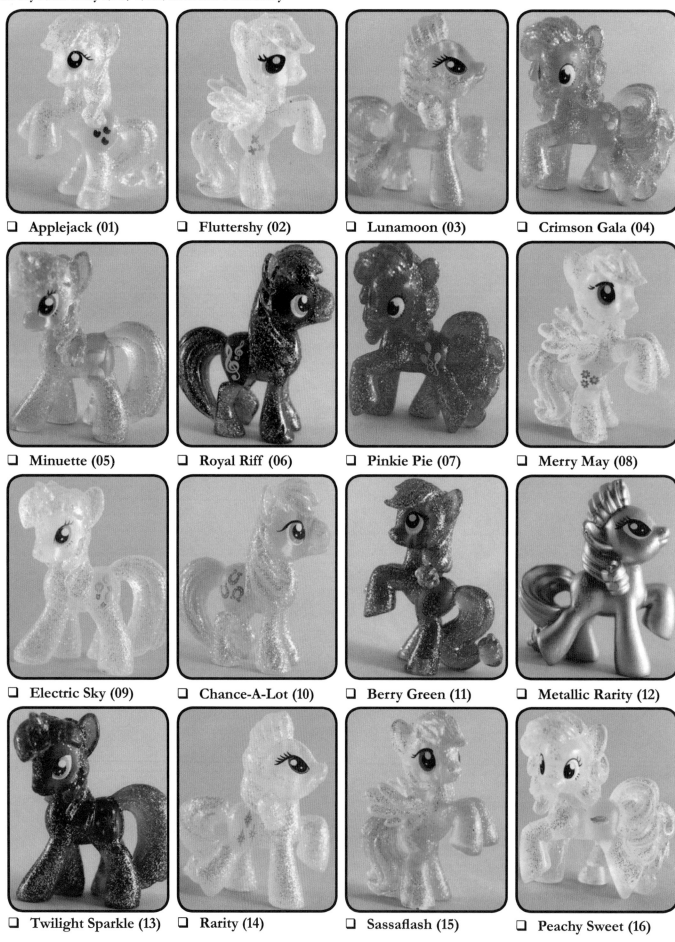

- Applejack (01)
- Fluttershy (02)
- Lunamoon (03)
- Crimson Gala (04)
- Minuette (05)
- Royal Riff (06)
- Pinkie Pie (07)
- Merry May (08)
- Electric Sky (09)
- Chance-A-Lot (10)
- Berry Green (11)
- Metallic Rarity (12)
- Twilight Sparkle (13)
- Rarity (14)
- Sassaflash (15)
- Peachy Sweet (16)

☐ Twilight Sky (17)

☐ Metallic Applejack (18)

☐ Rainbow Dash (19)

☐ Mosely Orange (20)

☐ Amethyst Star (21)

☐ Twilight Velvet (22)

☐ Shoeshine (23)

☐ Metallic Pinkie Pie (24)

Blind Bag Miniature Ponies
(fifth set)

The fifth set of Blind Bag Miniature Ponies came in yellow bags with Princess Cadance on the front. This set included three special Princess Ponies: Princesses Celestia, Cadance, and Luna. Though originally earth ponies in their full sized early 2000 releases, Island Rainbow, Flippity Flop, Gardenia Glow, Cinnamon Breeze, Golden Delicious, Ribbon Wishes and Forsythia all appeared as unicorns in this set while Breezie and Skywishes were now pegasus ponies. Island Rainbow's body color also switched from orange to pink while both Golden Delicious and Forsythia chagned hair and body colors. The collector's cards from this set are featured in the appendix.

☐ Twilight Sparkle (01)

☐ Princess Cadance (02)

☐ Sunny Rays (03)

☐ Junebug (04)

❑ Breezie (05) ❑ Island Rainbow (06) ❑ Princess Luna (07) ❑ Sapphire Shores (08)

❑ Rainbow Dash (09) ❑ Flippity Flop (10) ❑ Gardenia Glow (11) ❑ Skywishes (12)

❑ Trixie Lunamoon (13) ❑ Diamond Rose (14) ❑ Cinnamon Breeze (15) ❑ Ploomette (16)

❑ Golden Delicious (17) ❑ Ribbon Wishes (18) ❑ Princess Celestia (19) ❑ Fluttershy (20)

❑ Forsythia (21)

❑ Flitter Heart (22)

❑ Rainbow Wishes (23)

❑ Lyra Heartstrings (24)

Blind Bag Miniature Ponies
(sixth set)

The sixth set of Blind Bag Miniature Ponies came in purple and blue Crystal Empire bags. This set included three special ponies with three dimensional gem symbols. The collector's cards from this set are featured in the appendix.

❑ Pinkie Pie (01)

❑ Fluttershy (02)

❑ 3D Gem Twilight
Sparkle (03)

❑ Rainbow Dash (04)

❑ Rarity (05)

❑ Applejack (06)

❑ Minnuette (07)

❑ Roseluck (08)

❑ **3D Gem Trixie Lunamoon II (09)**

❑ **3D Gem Velvet Twilight (10)**

❑ **Mosely Orange (11)**

❑ **Berry Green (12)**

❑ **Merry May (13)**

❑ **Cherry Spices II (14)**

❑ **Electric Sky (15)**

❑ **Crimson Gala (16)**

❑ **Amethyst Star (17)**

❑ **Twilight Sky (18)**

❑ **Sassaflash (19)**

❑ **Magnet Bolt (20)**

❑ **Royal Riff (21)**

❑ **Peachy Sweet (22)**

❑ **Chance-A-Lot (23)**

❑ **Shoeshine (24)**

Friendship Celebration Collection

This Toys R Us Exclusive set included Miniature Ponies packaged with a variety of accessories. Ponies in this set were also available as part of the Blind Bag Miniature set 1 and Blind Bag Miniature set 2. The Friendship Celebration Collection was part of the Pony Friends Forever (P.F.F) line at Toys R Us stores.

- ❑ **Sweetie Swirl**
- ❑ **Firecracker Burst**
- ❑ Red pizza box
- ❑ Yellow pizza
- ❑ Pizza slice on plate
- ❑ Orange drink

- ❑ **Sugar Grape**
- ❑ **Lulu Luck**
- ❑ Blue book
- ❑ Pink teddy bear
- ❑ Pink popcorn box

- ❑ **Lily Blossom**
- ❑ **Bumblesweet**
- ❑ Picnic blanket (cardboard)
- ❑ Blue picnic basket
- ❑ Pink bunny friend
- ❑ Green drink
- ❑ Bananas and apple

- ❑ **Rainbow Flash**
- ❑ **Sweetie Blue**
- ❑ Pink gift box
- ❑ Pink balloons
- ❑ Purple cake slice on green plate

- ❑ **Lemon Hearts**
- ❑ **Pepperdance**
- ❑ Green drum set
- ❑ Pink keyboard

- ❑ **Blossomforth**
- ❑ **Flower Wishes**
- ❑ Pink table
- ❑ Pink teapot
- ❑ 2 yellow teacups with saucers
- ❑ White muffins

Miniature Collections

Each themed collections set contained three Miniature Ponies. While the Mane 6 ponies and McIntosh, whose name is spelled without the "a" from this point forward, are all reissues, there were several new characters introduced in this set.

Apple Family Set
- ❑ Granny Smith
- ❑ Big McIntosh
- ❑ Applejack

Cloudsdale Set
- ❑ Rainbow Dash
- ❑ Gilda the Griffon
- ❑ Wonder Bolts pony

Pony Wedding Set
- ❑ Shining Armor
- ❑ Princess Cadance
- ❑ Twilight Sparkle

Spa Pony Set
- ❑ Lotus Blossom
- ❑ Zecora
- ❑ Pinkie Pie

Class of Cutie Marks
- ❑ Diamond Dazzle Tiara
- ❑ Apple Bloom
- ❑ Applejack

Famous Friends Set
- ❑ Rarity
- ❑ Photo Finish
- ❑ Hoity Toity

Pinkie Pie & Friends Mini Collection

Available exclusively at Walmart stores as part of their Pony Power line, this set consisted of twelve ponies. Though originally earth ponies in their full sized early 2000 releases, Kiwi Tart, Seascape, Waterfire, Pick-a-Lily and Rainbow Swirl were now unicorns while Star Dasher, Dainty Daisy, and Periwinkle changed to pegasus ponies. The Mane 6 ponies are identical to their Blind Bag releases. The collector's cards from this set are featured in the appendix.

❑ **Rainbow Dash**

❑ **Pinkie Pie**

❑ **Kiwi Tart**

❑ **Seascape**

❑ **Star Dasher**   ❑ **Dainty Daisy**   ❑ **Periwinkle**   ❑ **Applejack**

❑ **Rarity**

❑ **Waterfire**

❑ **Pick-a-Lily**

❑ **Rainbow Swirl**

Playhouse Puzzles

These three different Playhouse Puzzle sets, each containing a Miniature Pony, allowed you to piece together a puzzle play mat.

❑ **Pinkie Pie**
❑ **Twilight Sparkle**
❑ **Fluttershy**
(not pictured)

Pony Rainbow Collection

Available exclusively at Target stores as part of their Crystal Empire line, this set included seven different Miniature Ponies, each representing a different color of the rainbow.

❑ **Pinkie Pie**
❑ **Applejack**
❑ **Fluttershy**
❑ **Emerald Ray**
❑ **Rainbow Dash**
❑ **Twilight Sparkle**
❑ **Rarity**

Funko Vinyl My Little Ponies

Sold exclusively at Hot Topic and specialty stores in 2012, these two ponies were the first from Funko, a Hasbro licensee. Each pony has molded hair and was packaged as a "vinyl collectible." The Funko Vinyl Ponies stand 5 inches high. While the grey pegasus pony is sometimes called "Derpy" or "Ditzy Doo" by fans of *My Little Pony: Friendship is Magic*, she has no official name.

❑ **Rainbow Dash**   ❑ **Grey Pegasus**

2012 McDonald's Ponies

In 2012, McDonald's restaurants offered My Little Pony toys in their Happy Meals. This set included eight ponies that appeared in *My Little Pony: Friendship is Magic*. Each pony was packaged with a clip that attached to the pony's head.

❑ **Applejack**
❑ Red clip
❑ **Cheerilee**
❑ Green clip
❑ **Fluttershy**
❑ Green clip
❑ **Lily Blossom**
❑ Pink clip
❑ **Pinkie Pie**
❑ Pink clip
❑ **Rainbow Dash**
❑ Orange clip
❑ **Rarity**
❑ Blue clip
❑ **Twilight Sparkle**
❑ Purple clip

So Soft Newborns

Soft and huggable, these battery operated So Soft Newborns spoke a variety of phrases when you squeezed their foot. Spike said several phrases including his name, "Did I miss snack time?" and "I'm hungry, " while Rainbow Dash yawned and said "I'm sleepy." and "I love to snuggle."

❑ **Spike the Dragon**
❑ Yellow baby bottle

❑ **Rainbow Dash**
❑ Pink pacifier

Princess Cadance Animated Storyteller

This huggable plush version of Princess Cadance's mouth moved as she told stories and sang songs. Packaged with four story books, several easy to use buttons on her front legs controlled her storytelling. Princess Cadance was battery operated and measured 12 inches high.

❑ **Princess Cadance**
❑ *The Wedding Invitation* storybook
❑ *Wedding Preparations* storybook
❑ *Twilight & Cadance* storybook
❑ *The Best Wedding Ever* storybook

My Little Pony Plush

In 2012, a collection of three large 10 inch plush ponies was available exclusively at Wal-Mart stores.

❑ **10" Pinkie Pie**

❑ **10" Rainbow Dash**

❑ **10" Twilight Sparkle**

Later this same year, Funrise Toys, a Hasbro licensee, released three smaller 5 inch plush ponies.

❑ **5" Pinkie Pie**
❑ **5" Rainbow Dash**
❑ **5" Twilight Sparkle**

Trading Cards

The Blind Bags series added a new element to My Little Pony collecting by introducing trading cards that came with each pony. This appendix offers a closer look at these cards.

2010 Ponyville Blind Bag Ponies and Mermaids

PINKIE PIE
- is everyone's best friend!
- a beaucoup d'amies !
- möchte deine beste Freundin sein!
- jes la mejor amiga de todas!
- é a melhor amiga de todas!
- è la miglior amica di tutti!
- is je beste vriendinnetje!
- är allas bästa vän!
- er bedste ven med alle!
- είναι η καλύτερη φίλη!
- jest najlepszą przyjaciółką!
- herkesin dostu!

PINKIE PIE
- is everyone's best friend!
- a beaucoup d'amies !
- möchte deine beste Freundin sein!
- jes la mejor amiga de todas!
- é a melhor amiga de todas!
- è la miglior amica di tutti!
- is je beste vriendinnetje!
- är allas bästa vän!
- er bedste ven med alle!
- είναι η καλύτερη φίλη!
- jest najlepszą przyjaciółką!
- herkesin dostu!

RAINBOW DASH
- is a real glamour girl!
- adore la mode !
- ist ein echtes Glamour-Girl!
- tiene mucho glamour!
- é uma miúda cheia de estilo!
- è una ragazza molto alla moda!
- is een echt meisje-meisje!
- är en riktig glamourtjej!
- er en rigtig glamourpige!
- είναι μία κολλονή!
- jest prawdziwą elegantką!
- gerçekten çok sevimli bir Kız!

SCOOTALOO
- loves playing games!
- adore jouer !
- spielt so gerne Spiele!
- le encanta jugar!
- adora jogar jogos!
- ama giocare!
- is dol op spelletjes doen!
- tycker om att spela spel!
- elsker at spille spil!
- λατρεύει να παίζει παιχνίδια!
- lubi gry i zabawy!
- oyun oynamayı çok seviyor!

CHEERILEE
- loves to read!
- adore lire !
- liest gerne Geschichten!
- le encanta leer!
- le piace leggere!
- houdt van lezen!
- älskar att läsa!
- elsker at læse!
- λατρεύει το διάβασμα!
- uwielbia czytać!
- Kitap okumaya bayılıyor!

TOOLA-ROOLA
- loves arts and crafts!
- adore l'art et les travaux manuels !
- malt und bastelt gerne!
- le encantan las manualidades!
- adora desenhar e pintar!
- ama disegnare e dipingere!
- is dol op knutselen en versieren!
- älskar att måla och pyssla!
- elsker at male og lave ting selv!
- λατρεύει τα καλλιτεχνικά!
- uwielbia sztukę i rękodzieło!
- el işleri yapmaya bayılıyor!

STARSONG
- loves to sing and dance!
- adore chanter et danser !
- singt und tanzt gerne!
- le encanta cantar y bailar!
- adora cantar e dançar!
- ama cantare e ballare!
- is dol op zingen en dansen!
- tycker om att sjunga och dansa!
- elsker at synge og danse!
- λατρεύει το τραγούδι και το χορό!
- lubi śpiewać i tańczyć!
- şarkı söyleyip dans etmeye bayılıyor!

STARSONG
- loves to sing and dance!
- adore chanter et danser !
- singt und tanzt gerne!
- le encanta cantar y bailar!
- adora cantar e dançar!
- ama cantare e ballare!
- is dol op zingen en dansen!
- tycker om att sjunga och dansa!
- elsker at synge og danse!
- λατρεύει το τραγούδι και το χορό!
- lubi śpiewać i tańczyć!
- şarkı söyleyip dans etmeye bayılıyor!

PINKIE PIE keeps her pony friends laughing and smiling all day! Cheerful and playful, she always looks on the bright side.

APPLEJACK is honest, friendly and sweet to the core! She loves to be outside, and her friends know they can always count on her.

RAINBOW DASH loves to fly as fast as she can! She is always ready to play a game, go on an adventure, or help out one of her friends.

RARITY knows how to add sparkle to any outfit! She loves to give her friends advice on the latest pony fashions and hairstyles.

TWILIGHT SPARKLE tries to find the answer to every question! Whether studying a book or spending time with friends, she always learns something new!

FLUTTERSHY is a kind and gentle pony with a big heart. She likes to take care of others, especially her little animal friends!

SUGAR GRAPE loves to read stories. Fairy tales are her favorite!

LILY BLOSSOM is known for being graceful when she flies, but she is just as elegant on all four hooves!

MINTY loves to celebrate holidays with her friends! Her favorite season is winter.

9

BUMBLESWEET is very polite! She loves to talk to everypony and always has something nice to say.

10

FIZZYPOP loves to blow bubbles as big as she can, but her favorite part is watching them pop!

11

FLOWER WISHES has a beautiful garden. She grows flowers in every color of the rainbow!

12

ROSELUCK loves to pick pretty flowers and wear them in her hair!

13

SWEETIE BLUE loves to decorate sweet treats with sprinkles and fun toppings!

14

PEPPERDANCE loves to race with her friends! She is always ready for a challenge.

15

LEMON HEARTS is loving and kind! She always takes time to show her friends how much she cares.

16

153

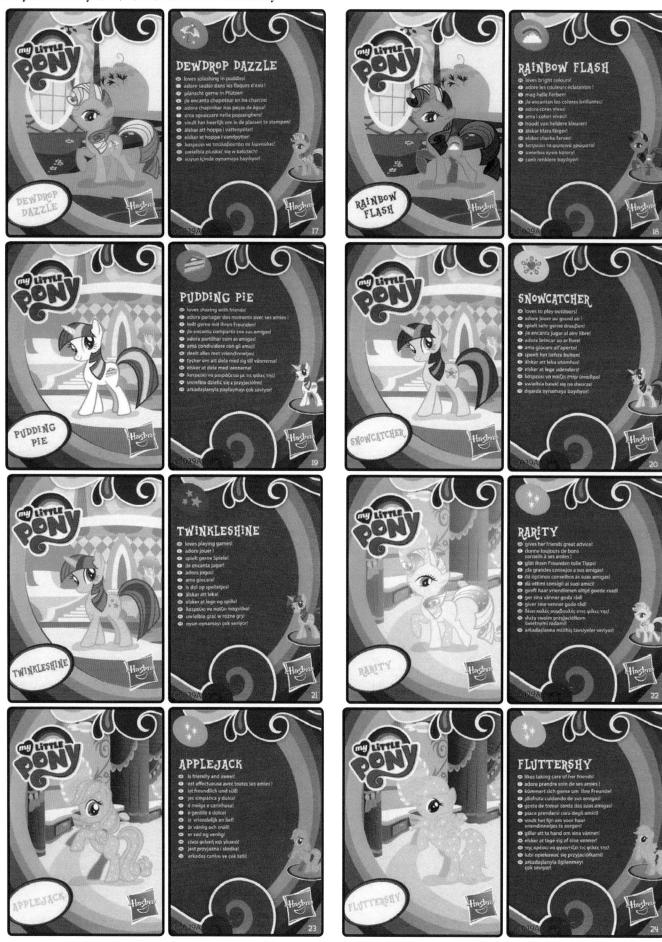

DEWDROP DAZZLE
- loves splashing in puddles!
- adore sauter dans les flaques d'eau !
- planscht gerne in Pfützen!
- ¡le encanta chapotear en los charcos!
- adora chapinhar nas poças de água!
- ama squazzare nelle pozzanghere!
- vindt het heerlijk om in de plassen te stampen!
- älskar att hoppa i vattenpölar!
- elsker at hoppe i vandpytter!
- λατρεύει να τσαλαβουτάει σε λιμνούλες!
- uwielbia pluskać się w kałużach!
- suyun içinde oynamaya bayılıyor!

17

RAINBOW FLASH
- loves bright colours!
- adore les couleurs éclatantes !
- mag helle Farben!
- ¡le encantan los colores brillantes!
- adora cores vivas!
- ama i colori vivaci!
- houdt van heldere kleuren!
- älskar klara färger!
- elsker stærke farver!
- λατρεύει τα φωτεινά χρώματα!
- uwielbia żywe kolory!
- canlı renklere bayılıyor!

18

PUDDING PIE
- loves sharing with friends!
- adore partager des moments avec ses amies !
- teilt sehr gerne mit ihren Freunden!
- ¡le encanta compartir con sus amigas!
- adora partilhar com as amigas!
- ama condividere con gli amici!
- deelt heel graag met vriendinnetjes!
- tycker om att dela med sig till vännerna!
- elsker at dele med vennerne!
- λατρεύει να μοιράζεται με τις φίλες της!
- uwielbia dzielić się z przyjaciółmi!
- arkadaşlarıyla paylaşmayı çok seviyor!

19

SNOWCATCHER
- loves to play outdoors!
- adore jouer au grand air !
- spielt sehr gerne draußen!
- ¡le encanta jugar al aire libre!
- adora brincar ao ar livre!
- ama giocare all'aperto!
- speelt het liefste buiten!
- älskar att leka utomhus!
- elsker at lege udendørs!
- λατρεύει να παίζει στην ύπαιθρο!
- uwielbia bawić się na dworze!
- dışarda oynamaya bayılıyor!

20

TWINKLESHINE
- loves playing games!
- adore jouer !
- spielt gerne Spiele!
- ¡le encanta jugar!
- adora jogos!
- ama giocare!
- is dol op spelletjes!
- älskar att leka!
- elsker at lege og spille!
- λατρεύει να παίζει παιχνίδια!
- uwielbia grać w różne gry!
- oyun oynamayı çok seviyor!

21

RARITY
- gives her friends great advice!
- donne toujours de bons conseils à ses amies !
- gibt ihren Freunden tolle Tipps!
- ¡da grandes consejos a sus amigas!
- dá óptimos conselhos às suas amigas!
- dà ottimi consigli ai suoi amici!
- geeft haar vriendinnen altijd goede raad!
- ger sina vänner goda råd!
- giver sine venner gode råd!
- δίνει καλές συμβουλές στις φίλες της!
- służy swoim przyjaciółkom świetnymi radami!
- arkadaşlarına müthiş tavsiyeler veriyor!

22

APPLEJACK
- is friendly and sweet!
- est affectueuse avec toutes ses amies !
- ist freundlich und süß!
- ¡es simpática y dulce!
- é meiga e carinhosa!
- è gentile e dolce!
- is vriendelijk en lief!
- är vänlig och snäll!
- er sød og venlig!
- είναι φιλική και γλυκιά!
- jest przyjazna i słodka!
- arkadaş canlısı ve çok tatlı!

23

FLUTTERSHY
- likes taking care of her friends!
- adore prendre soin de ses amies !
- kümmert sich gerne um ihre Freunde!
- ¡disfruta cuidando de sus amigas!
- gosta de tomar conta das suas amigas!
- piace prendersi cura degli amici!
- vindt het fijn om voor haar vriendinnetjes te zorgen!
- gillar att ta hand om sina vänner!
- elsker at tage sig af sine venner!
- της αρέσει να φροντίζει τις φίλες της!
- lubi opiekować się przyjaciółkami!
- arkadaşlarıyla ilgilenmeyi çok seviyor!

24

2011 Pony Collection Set (Toys R Us Exclusive)

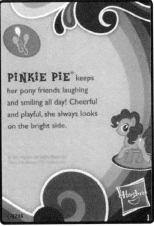

PINKIE PIE keeps her pony friends laughing and smiling all day! Cheerful and playful, she always looks on the bright side.

1

APPLEJACK is honest, friendly and sweet to the core! She loves to be outside, and her friends know they can always count on her.

2

RAINBOW DASH loves to fly as fast as she can! She is always ready to play a game, go on an adventure, or help out one of her friends.

3

RARITY knows how to add sparkle to any outfit! She loves to give her friends advice on the latest pony fashions and hairstyles.

4

TWILIGHT SPARKLE tries to find the answer to every question! Whether studying a book or spending time with friends, she always learns something new!

5

FLUTTERSHY is a kind and gentle pony with a big heart. She likes to take care of others, especially her little animal friends!

6

COCONUT CREAM makes delicious pies to share at parties and picnics. The only thing she won't share is the secret ingredient!

7

SWEETSONG has a beautiful voice! She loves singing songs for her friends, especially when they sing along.

8

157

SKYWISHES has big dreams and never gives up. She loves wishing on stars, especially for her friends!

9

GARDENIA GLOW knows how to make any garden grow! All it takes is a little love and care, and some help from her friends.

10

BEACHBERRY loves spending time at the beach! Soaking up sunshine and relaxing with her friends, she always has a great time!

11

PEACHY PIE loves baking sweet treats for her friends! She's always testing out new recipes for them to try.

12

2012 Blind Bag Set 3 (Cards in this set feature only one of four possible fronts.)

2012 Blind Bag Set 4 (Cards in this set feature only one of four possible fronts.)

2012 Blind Bag Set 5 (Cards in this set feature only one of four possible fronts.)

PRINCESS LUNA

- 🇬🇧 stays up late!
- 🇫🇷 se couche toujours tard !
- 🇩🇪 bleibt auf bis tief in die Nacht!
- 🇪🇸 ¡se acuesta muy tarde!
- 🇹🇷 fica acordada até tarde!
- 🇮🇹 sta alzata fino a tardi!
- 🇳🇱 houdt van laat opblijven!
- 🇸🇪 går och lägger sig sent!
- 🇩🇰 er længe oppe!
- 🇬🇷 μένει ξύπνια ως αργά!
- 🇵🇱 późno chodzi spać!
- 🇹🇷 gece geç yatıyor!
- 🇷🇺 не ложится спать допоздна!

C-029A · 7

SAPPHIRE SHORES

- 🇬🇧 is quietly kind.
- 🇫🇷 est gentille et calme.
- 🇩🇪 ist ruhig und freundlich.
- 🇪🇸 es discreta y amable.
- 🇮🇹 é discreta e simpática.
- 🇵🇹 è spontaneamente gentile.
- 🇳🇱 is rustig vriendelijk.
- 🇸🇪 är vänlig i tysthet.
- 🇩🇰 er stille og venlig.
- 🇬🇷 είναι ήσυχα ευγενική.
- 🇵🇱 jest cicha i dobra.
- 🇹🇷 yumuşak ve nazik.
- 🇷🇺 спокойна.

C-029A · 8

RAINBOW DASH

- 🇬🇧 loves to help her friends!
- 🇫🇷 aime aider ses amies !
- 🇩🇪 liebt es, ihren Freunden zu helfen!
- 🇪🇸 ¡le encanta ayudar a sus amigas!
- 🇹🇷 adora ajudar as amigas!
- 🇮🇹 ama aiutare i suoi amici!
- 🇳🇱 vindt het fijn om haar vriendinnetjes te helpen!
- 🇸🇪 hjälper gärna sina vänner!
- 🇩🇰 elsker at hjælpe sine venner!
- 🇬🇷 λατρεύει να βοηθάει τις φίλες της!
- 🇵🇱 uwielbia pomagać swoim przyjaciółkom!
- 🇹🇷 çok seviyor!
- 🇷🇺 любит помогать своим друзьям!

C-029A · 9

FLIPPITY FLOP

- 🇬🇧 giggles all day!
- 🇫🇷 s'amuse toute la journée !
- 🇩🇪 kichert den ganzen Tag!
- 🇪🇸 ¡se ríe durante todo el día!
- 🇹🇷 ri o dia todo!
- 🇮🇹 ride tutto il giorno!
- 🇳🇱 lacht de hele dag!
- 🇸🇪 fnittrar hela dagen!
- 🇩🇰 griner hele dagen!
- 🇬🇷 γελάει όλη μέρα!
- 🇵🇱 caly dzień się śmieje!
- 🇹🇷 bütün gün gülüyor!
- 🇷🇺 весь день хихикает!

C-029A · 10

GARDENIA GLOW

- 🇬🇧 makes gardens grow!
- 🇫🇷 prend soin de son jardin !
- 🇩🇪 verschönert jeden Garten!
- 🇪🇸 ¡cultiva jardines!
- 🇹🇷 faz os jardins florir!
- 🇮🇹 fa giardinaggio!
- 🇳🇱 laat alles groeien en bloeien!
- 🇸🇪 har gröna fingrar!
- 🇩🇰 får planterne til at gro!
- 🇬🇷 κάνει τους κήπους να μεγαλώνουν!
- 🇵🇱 jest świetną ogrodniczką!
- 🇹🇷 bahçelerle ilgileniyor!
- 🇷🇺 ухаживает за садом!

C-029A · 11

SKYWISHES

- 🇬🇧 has big dreams.
- 🇫🇷 a de grands rêves.
- 🇩🇪 hat große Träume.
- 🇪🇸 tiene grandes sueños.
- 🇹🇷 tem grandes sonhos.
- 🇮🇹 ha grandi sogni.
- 🇳🇱 heeft grote dromen.
- 🇸🇪 har storslagna drömmar.
- 🇩🇰 drømmer store dromme.
- 🇬🇷 έχει μεγάλα όνειρα.
- 🇵🇱 ma wielkie marzenia.
- 🇹🇷 büyük hayalleri var.
- 🇷🇺 мечтательная.

C-029A · 12

MY LITTLE PONY

TRIXIE LULAMOON
DIAMOND ROSE
CINNAMON BREEZE
PLOOMETTE
GOLDEN DELICIOUS
RIBBON WISHES

WWW.MYLITTLEPONY.COM

TRIXIE LULAMOON

- 🇬🇧 likes showing off!
- 🇫🇷 adore se montrer !
- 🇩🇪 zeigt sich gerne!
- 🇪🇸 ¡le gusta presumir!
- 🇹🇷 adora dar nas vistas!
- 🇮🇹 le piace mettersi in mostra!
- 🇳🇱 steelt de show!
- 🇸🇪 älskar att visa upp sig!
- 🇩🇰 kan lide at vise sig!
- 🇬🇷 της αρέσει να κάνει επίδειξη!
- 🇵🇱 lubi się popisywać!
- 🇹🇷 hava atmayı seviyor!
- 🇷🇺 любит красоваться!

C-029A · 13

DIAMOND ROSE

- 🇬🇧 sparkles with fun!
- 🇫🇷 brille de mille feux !
- 🇩🇪 strahlt vor Glück!
- 🇪🇸 ¡brilla de felicidad!
- 🇹🇷 brilha com piada!
- 🇮🇹 brilla di felicità!
- 🇳🇱 glinstert van de pret!
- 🇸🇪 glittrar av glädje!
- 🇩🇰 bobler af glæde!
- 🇬🇷 λάμπει με διασκέδαση!
- 🇵🇱 promienieje radością!
- 🇹🇷 neşe saçıyor!
- 🇷🇺 излучает радость!

C-029A · 14

CINNAMON BREEZE

- 🇬🇧 has a warm heart.
- 🇫🇷 a un grand coeur.
- 🇩🇪 hat ein gutes Herz.
- 🇪🇸 tiene un gran corazón.
- 🇹🇷 tem um coração caloroso.
- 🇮🇹 ha un cuore d'oro.
- 🇳🇱 is heel erg lief.
- 🇸🇪 har ett varmt hjärta.
- 🇩🇰 har et varmt hjerte.
- 🇬🇷 έχει ζεστή καρδιά.
- 🇵🇱 ma cieple serce.
- 🇹🇷 sıcacık bir kalbi var.
- 🇷🇺 добросердечная.

C-029A · 15

PLOOMETTE

- 🇬🇧 has pretty wings!
- 🇫🇷 a des ailes splendides !
- 🇩🇪 hat schöne Flügel!
- 🇪🇸 ¡tiene unas alas preciosas!
- 🇹🇷 tem asas bonitas!
- 🇮🇹 ha ali leggiadre!
- 🇳🇱 heeft prachtige vleugeltjes!
- 🇸🇪 har vackra vingar!
- 🇩🇰 har kønne vinger!
- 🇬🇷 έχει όμορφα φτερά!
- 🇵🇱 ma piękne skrzydła!
- 🇹🇷 güzel kanatları var!
- 🇷🇺 с милыми крылышками!

C-029A · 16

GOLDEN DELICIOUS

- 🇬🇧 loves acting!
- 🇫🇷 adore jouer la comédie !
- 🇩🇪 liebt die Schauspielerei!
- 🇪🇸 ¡le encanta actuar!
- 🇹🇷 adora fazer coisas!
- 🇮🇹 ama l'azione!
- 🇳🇱 speelt graag toneel!
- 🇸🇪 älskar att spela teater!
- 🇩🇰 elsker at optræde!
- 🇬🇷 λατρεύει την υποκριτική!
- 🇵🇱 uwielbia odgrywanie ról!
- 🇹🇷 oyunculuğu seviyor!
- 🇷🇺 любит быть деятельной!

C-029A · 17

RIBBON WISHES

- 🇬🇧 loves making wishes!
- 🇫🇷 adore faire des voeux !
- 🇩🇪 wünscht sich gerne etwas!
- 🇪🇸 ¡le encanta pedir deseos!
- 🇹🇷 adora esprimere desideri!
- 🇮🇹 vindt het heerlijk om iets te wensen!
- 🇸🇪 älskar att önska sig saker!
- 🇩🇰 elsker at ønske noget!
- 🇬🇷 λατρεύει να κάνει ευχές!
- 🇵🇱 uwielbia wymyślać nowe życzenia!
- 🇹🇷 dilek tutmayı seviyor!
- 🇷🇺 любит загадывать желания!

C-029A · 18

MY LITTLE PONY

PRINCESS CELESTIA
FORSYTHIA
FLUTTERSHY
FLITTER HEART
RAINBOW WISHES
LYRA HEARTSTRINGS

WWW.MYLITTLEPONY.COM

PRINCESS CELESTIA

- 🇬🇧 is a magical pony!
- 🇫🇷 est un poney magique !
- 🇩🇪 ist ein magisches Pony!
- 🇪🇸 ¡es una amiga pony mágica!
- 🇹🇷 é uma pony mágica!
- 🇮🇹 è un pony magico!
- 🇳🇱 is een sprookjesachtige pony!
- 🇸🇪 är en magisk pony!
- 🇩🇰 er en magisk pony!
- 🇬🇷 είναι ένα μαγικό πόνι!
- 🇵🇱 jest czarodziejskim kucykiem!
- 🇹🇷 sihirli bir pony!
- 🇷🇺 сказочная пони!

C-029A · 19

FLUTTERSHY

- 🇬🇧 blushes often.
- 🇫🇷 rougit souvent.
- 🇩🇪 ist sehr schüchtern.
- 🇪🇸 se sonroja a menudo.
- 🇹🇷 fica envergonhada muitas vezes.
- 🇮🇹 arrossisce spesso.
- 🇳🇱 bloost heel vaak.
- 🇸🇪 rodnar ofta.
- 🇩🇰 rødmer let.
- 🇬🇷 κοκκινίζει συχνά.
- 🇵🇱 często się rumieni.
- 🇹🇷 çok utangaç.
- 🇷🇺 часто краснеет.

C-029A · 20

FORSYTHIA

- loves spring flowers!
- adore les fleurs du printemps!
- liebt Frühlingsblumen!
- ¡le encantan las flores de primavera!
- adora as flores da Primavera!
- ama i fiori primaverili!
- houdt van lentebloemen!
- älskar vårblommor!
- elsker forårsblomster!
- λατρεύει τα ανοιξιάτικα λουλούδια!
- uwielbia wiosenne kwiaty!
- bahar çiçeklerini seviyor!
- любит весенние цветы!

21

FLITTER HEART

- lets her dreams soar!
- se laisse porter par ses rêves !
- lässt ihren Träumen freien Lauf!
- ¡es una soñadora!
- é uma sonhadora!
- lascia che i suoi sogni si avverino!
- droomt de allermooiste dromen!
- älskar att drömma sig bort!
- elsker at drømme sig væk!
- αφήνει τα όνειρά της ελεύθερα!
- uwielbia marzyć!
- hayal kurmaya bayılıyor!
- предается мечтам!

22

RAINBOW WISHES

- chases rainbows!
- part à la chasse aux arcs-en-ciel !
- jagt dem Regenbogen hinterher!
- ¡persigue arco iris!
- persegue os arco-íris!
- rincorre l'arcobaleno!
- zit achter de regenboog aan!
- jagar regnbågar!
- jagter regnbuer!
- κυνηγάει ουράνια τόξα!
- szuka tęczy!
- gökkuşaklarını kovalıyor!
- охотится за радугой!

23

LYRA HEARTSTRINGS

- loves to play!
- adore jouer !
- spielt gerne!
- ¡le encanta jugar!
- adora brincar!
- ama giocare!
- houdt van spelen!
- älskar att leka!
- elsker at lege!
- λατρεύει να παίζει!
- uwielbia się bawić!
- oyun oynamayı çok seviyor!
- любит играть!

24

2012 Blind Bag Set 6 (Cards in this set feature only one of four possible fronts.)

WWW.MYLITTLEPONY.COM

PINKIE PIE

keeps her friends laughing and smiling all day!

01

FLUTTERSHY

likes taking care of her friends!

02

TWILIGHT SPARKLE

loves learning with her friends!

03

RAINBOW DASH

is always ready to help her friends.

04

RARITY

loves to give her friends great advice!

05

APPLEJACK

is honest, friendly and sweet to the core!

06

WWW.MYLITTLEPONY.COM

MINUETTE

is always on time with the help of some magic!

07

ROSELUCK

loves to pick pretty flowers and wear them in her hair!

08

TRIXIE LULAMOON

is great at magic tricks!

09

TWILIGHT VELVET

loves writing stories about adventures!

10

MOSELY ORANGE™
loves to have fancy parties!
C-029A   11

BERRY GREEN™
has lots of friends she can always count on!
C-029A   12

WWW.MYLITTLEPONY.COM

MERRY MAY™
loves all flowers, especially spring daisies!
C-029A   13

CHERRY SPICES™
loves to bake and make up yummy recipes!
C-029A   14

ELECTRIC SKY™
has so many smart ideas to share!
C-029A   15

CRIMSON GALA™
gives everyone treats when she visits!
C-029A   16

AMETHYST STAR™
loves to dance when she hears music!
C-029A   17

TWILIGHT SKY™
loves to play guessing games with friends!
C-029A   18

WWW.MYLITTLEPONY.COM

SASSAFLASH™
loves watching clouds blow across the sky!
C-029A   19

MAGNET BOLT™
attracts a lot of attention wherever she goes!
C-029A   20

ROYAL RIFF™
makes up songs to sing together with friends!
C-029A   21

PEACHY SWEET™
is always smiling wherever she goes!
C-029A   22

CHANCE-A-LOT™
is always cheerful and trying new things!
C-029A   23

SHOESHINE™
is understanding and listens to her friends!
C-029A   24

2012 Pinkie Pie & Friends Mini Collection (Walmart Exclusive)

PINKIE PIE keeps her pony friends laughing and smiling all day! Cheerful and playful, she always looks on the bright side.

APPLEJACK is honest, friendly and sweet to the core! She loves to be outside, and her friends know they can always count on her.

RAINBOW DASH loves to fly as fast as she can! She is always ready to play a game, go on an adventure, or help out one of her friends.

RARITY knows how to add sparkle to any outfit! She loves to give her friends advice on the latest pony fashions and hairstyles.

TWILIGHT SPARKLE tries to find the answer to every question! Whether studying a book or spending time with friends, she always learns something new!

FLUTTERSHY is a kind and gentle pony with a big heart. She likes to take care of others, especially her little animal friends!

COCONUT CREAM makes delicious pies to share at parties and picnics. The only thing she won't share is the secret ingredient!

SWEETSONG has a beautiful voice! She loves singing songs for her friends, especially when they sing along.

SKYWISHES has big dreams and never gives up. She loves wishing on stars, especially for her friends!

9

GARDENIA GLOW knows how to make any garden grow! All it takes is a little love and care, and some help from her friends.

10

BEACHBERRY loves spending time at the beach! Soaking up sunshine and relaxing with her friends, she always has a great time!

11

PEACHY PIE loves baking sweet treats for her friends! She's always testing out new recipes for them to try.

12

Index

U

V

W

X

Y

Z

About the Author

Summer Hayes has been collecting My Little Ponies for as long as she can remember. Over the years, she has accumulated an extensive collection of ponies, accessories, and merchandise from all four generations and from multiple countries. Summer has been active in the My Little Pony collecting community for many years. She currently coordinates the MY LITTLE PONY Fair and Convention, an annual event celebrating My Little Pony and the people who collect them. Summer currently resides in southern Indiana with her husband, son, and their barky dogs. Visit Summer's blog for updates on her writing projects, MY LITTLE PONY Fair planning, and ramblings about all things My Little Pony.

She is also the author of the *The My Little Pony G1 Collector's Inventory, The My Little Pony G2 Collector's Inventory ,The My Little Pony G3 Collector's Inventory* and *The My Little Pony 2007-2008 Collector's Inventory.*

http://www.mylittleponycollector.blogspot.com

Twitter: @purplepajamas

24070169R00097

Made in the USA
Lexington, KY
04 July 2013